ARCHAEOLOGIST OF MORNING

ARCHAEOLOGIST OF MORNING

CHARLES OLSON

Cape Goliard Press
in association with
Grossman Publishers New York

© copyright Charles Olson 1970.

This first edition was designed, printed and published by Cape Goliard Press,
10a Fairhazel Gdns, London NW6.

Printed in Great Britain.

Acknowledgments are due to the following, who originally published these poems: The
Albuquerque Review, Aries Publications, Ark II/Moby 1, Artisan, Atlantic Monthly,
Before Your Very Eyes, Black Mountain College & Review, Black Sun Press, CIV/n,
City Lights Journal, Combustion, Contact, Evergreen Review, Vincent Ferrini, Floating
Bear, Four Winds, Gloucester Daily Times, Goad, Golden Goose, Harpers Bazaar,
Harpers Monthly Magazine, Imagi, Jargon, Knoedler, Magazine of Further Studies, Matter,
Measure, Montevallo Review, The Nation, Neon Obit, Neon/Supplement to Now, New
Directions Annual, Niagara Frontier Review, Origin, Outsider, Partisan Review, Poetry
(Chicago), Resuscitator, Right Angle, Set, Tuftonian Centennial Issue, Western Review,
White Rabbit Press, Wild Dog and Yugen. Twenty-one poems are reprinted with per-
mission of Grove Press, Inc.

The publishers wish to acknowledge and thank for their essential and selfless work on this
volume: Mr George Butterick, who gathered and discriminated; Mr Albert Glover, who
also gathered, and masterminded the present ordering; and Mr Peter Riley, who gathered
early. And of course the Big Man who still is.

Cover Illustration: Lingsberg rune stone, courtesy of the Swedish Embassy, London.

PS
3529
L655 A17
1970

UK SBN 206 61880 8

US SBN 670 13034 6

Library of Congress No. 70 135124

you islands

of men and girls

Lower Field—Enniscorthy

The sheep like soldiers
black leggings black face
lie boulders
in the pines' shade
at the field's sharp edge:
ambush and bivouac

A convocation of crows overhead
mucks
in their own mud and squawk
makes of the sky
a sty

A bee is deceived
takes the rot of a stump
for honeycomb

Two black snakes cross
in a flat spiral
the undisciplined path

Report: over all
the sun.

A Lion upon the Floor

Begin a song

Power and the abstract
distract a man
from his own gain

Begin a song of six cents

foul his eye
deprive his hand upon a nape and hips
of kiss beak claw
—a lion upon the floor

Sing a song

Let the salt in
begin
cut the heart open
the blood will run with sun
the wind will put the belly back
and the rain the roar below

Sing a song of six cents
sing a song of seven seas

The tall grass green
the muscle in the sea
an axe to cut a continent
an ox to walk a sky

Sing a song of six cents
sing a song of seven seas
give a girl to each man
to put him on his knees

Lion, spring!

Troilus

Love is not present now,
has flown
        is not a state so separate as we think
that men and women breed by kiss and glance
        no dance
outside the modes and figures of that trance,
the full intent

That love at least must live
is lie we practice to protect
What we inherit, breath;
unwilling to admit
the large wrongs bring
love also down to
death

Why should love live
when all that should enforce it fails
this side of meaning
              tearing off
what love alone is key to, form
that feature nature wore
before man turned her, woman, whore;
when matter stood so many objects clear
not use, delight the round of human year

Love is not love with end, with objects lost.
Means wither. Bodies, gestures fall.
                  All nature falls.
The path, are blown along the path papers, dust
cloth (strips which give no clue
dropped without care
picked up, lamely, at a dare)

The path, love is the path.
               And in the forest calls, calls!
We shall answer, find.
             But if love now is lust
or mere drift back
better we know, and say
we do not know the way

The way, love is
the way!

Only the Red Fox,
Only the Crow

You who come after us
you who can live when we are not
make much of love

You to whom the spring can return
when we will merely correlate a worm
enjoy the envy
in this blind glance

You who shall have the earth,
and one another,
the government of noon,
do not fail us, dance

We shall not know, but you
remember this: the two-edged worth
of loveliness
The night's for talking and for kissing

And when, on summer field
two horses run for joy
like figures on a beach
your mind will find us,
as we have found,
within its reach.

This, then, under the leaves
or under snow,
you who come after us,
we send you for envoy:
make most of love.

Pacific Lament

In memory of William Hickey, a member of the crew of the U.S.S.
Growler, lost at sea in February, 1944.

Black at that depth
turn, golden boy no more
white bone to bone, turn
hear who bore you weep
hear him who made you
deep there on ocean's floor
turn,
as waters stir;
turn, bone of man

Cold as a planet is
cold, beat of blood no more
the salt sea's course
along the bone jaw white
stir, boy, stir
motion without motion
stir, and hear
love come down

Down as you fell
sidewise, stair to green stair
without breath, down
the tumble of ocean
to find you, bone
cold and new among the ships
and men and fish askew.

You alone o golden boy no more
turn now and sleep
washed white by water
sleep in your black deep
by water out of which man came
to find his legs, arms, love, pain.
Sleep, boy, sleep
in older arms than hers,
rocked by an older father;
toss no more,
love;
sleep

In the Hills
South of Capernaum, Port

As salt, keep your savour
as light be not obscured.

The old commandments hold,
I would intensify them:

not to kill, yes, but also not without cause
to take anger
or to say Raca to your brother, or, thou fool

adultery, commit it not, nor even in your heart
nor put away your wife
saving for the cause of fornication

swear not, nor by earth, for it is God's footstool
nor by your head
for you cannot make one hair white or black

eye for eye, no. Give your enemy your coat
cheek also
and go two mile with him

The sun rises. And on the just and the unjust
the rain comes down.
The idea is to be perfect.

2

Nor sound the trumpet of what you do
be not public when you pray, nor repetitious
and when you fast
wear no long face.

The light of the body is the eye, let it be clear.

And be clear too concerning treasures and/or masters
any double allegiance. Take the natural for base
assume your nature as a bird his or the grass.
The life is more than meat, the body than clothes.

3

Nor judge, nor give what is holy to dogs
give gifts largely, as a father might
what man, if his son ask a fish, gives a snake?

Few find, but do you look for, enter, the narrow gate
Watch out for the false, the wide ones, frauds
Men do not gather grapes where thorns are
make wine with their feet in that place
find figs in thistles or tulips

The proposition is this:
a good tree and a rock
or
a foolish man, and sand.

   He taught them as one having authority.

Name-Day Night

*(for James Stathes, George Pistolas,
and Stephanos Radis)*

What it is to look into a human eye

men men what they are
who, of a sudden of a night in a room
a room not so different from this in which I sit
(along the floor circles of lamp light intersect),
start up, join hands, a kerchief joins them, their eyes follow
the pattern of their leader's feet their order,
they dance

what it is what it is to say wherein it lies

where beauty lies
                that men containeth
                                at this hour

Came 2 am the three men sang
one led (as in the dance) he of Peloponnesus
he sang of love, a narrative of man and maid
their meeting what the youth said
the night left out the morning, final stanza, key

then proudly (as he had danced) the Macedonian
he sang of war most hieratically; Turks defeated
and, at each turning of the song, pistols shot off

None sang of death. I marked then, and ask now
what light it is shines in their eyes, what source
their gusto hath
this name-day night these men of Greece disclose
their eyes shine from outside, take light, shine
from nature, partake her common force, shine
by addition, separation, what is cruel
are not monocular, shine
by death its recognition, multiply
by life its shorcoming, shine
these eyes of night their sons and daughters know not of

And the hour tells what it is
                      what delight it is
                                  that maketh modest man

The K

Take, then, my answer:
there is a tide in a man
moves him to his moon and,
though it drop him back
he works through ebb to mount
the run again and swell
to be tumescent I

The affairs of men remain a chief concern

We have come full circle.
I shall not see the year 2000
unless I stem straight from my father's mother,
break the fatal male small span.
If that is what the tarot pack proposed
I shall hang out some second story window
and sing, as she, one unheard liturgy

Assume I shall not.
Is it of such concern when what shall be
already is within the moonward sea?

Full circle: an end to romans, hippocrats and christians.
There! is a tide in the affairs of men to discern

Shallows and miseries shadows from the cross,
ecco men and dull copernican sun.
Our attention is simpler
The salts and minerals of the earth return
The night has a love for throwing its shadows around a man
a bridge, a horse, the gun, a grave.

The Moebius Strip

Upon a Moebius strip
materials and the weights of pain
their harmony

A man within himself upon an empty ground.
His head lay heavy on a huge right hand
itself a leopard on
his left and angled shoulder.
His back a stave, his side a hole into the bosom of a sphere.

His head passed down a sky (as suns the circle of a year).
His other shoulder, open side and thigh maintained,
by law of conservation of
the graveness of his center,
their clockwise fall.
Then he knew, so came to apogee
and earned and wore himself as amulet.

I saw another man lift up a woman in his arms
he helmeted, she naked too, protected as Lucrece by her alarms.
Her weight tore down his right and muscled thigh
but they in turn returned upon the left
to carry violence outcome in her eye.
It was his shoulder that sustained, the right,
bunched as by buttocks or by breasts,
and gave them back the leisure of their rape.

And three or four who danced,
so joined as triple-thighed and bowed and arrowed folk
who spilled their pleasure once as yoke
on stone-henge plain.
Their bare and lovely bodies sweep, in round
of viscera, of legs
of turned-out hip and glance, bound
each to other, nested eggs
of elements in trance.

Trinacria

Who fights behind a shield
Is separate, weak of the world
Is whirled by sons of self, sown
As teeth, a full armed crop
Sprung from no dream
No givers of a fleece
Who bring their dragon blood inside
Reality, half slain

There is a sword. If not so armed
A man will hide within himself
The armed man too, but battle
Is an outside thing, the field
Its own reward, reality

    Join sword and shield, yield
    Neither ground, contend
    And with one stroke behead
    The three, the enemy

    Then, like a Greek, emboss
    The shield with legs, and boast
    Of mighty ancestry.

The Green Man

Go, fool, and hatch of the air
a blue egg.
And the night will be there, the Twins
a different thing.

And you? can hang your plough
from a gold bough,
your tongue
on any branch,
and follow after.

Follow, fool, your stick and bag
and each furious cloud.
Let those who want to, chase a king.

And you who go when the green man comes
who leave your fields,
go as the dog goes at his heels
ahead, aside, and always after
be full of
loud laughter

    Of bitter work, and of folly
    cockatrice and cockolloly
    furiously sing!

These Days

whatever you have to say, leave
the roots on, let them
dangle

And the dirt

          just to make clear
          where they came from

The Story of an Olson, and Bad Thing

PART 1

Bad Thing came in the night, and, this time, ate away part of my
heart. Yet I endure, knowing no cure, because, as each is, I am
stubborn, the only difference the usual one, individual difference
(huge swedish teeth like my father's, whom god keeps, because he
was really in there, and smelled of violets, but it killed him in the
end, his stubbornness, literally it brought about his death. We are
such fools, these olson males, the way we go by, the way we live
up to, like liars, like strong-teethed men, the affections!)

I, too, waste (and this was certainly one thing I took warning from
his death, so help me god) waste out mortal strength. So I live, by
warning, in daily fear I'll not break down by the nerves, as my fellows
do, but by, as he did, the blood vessels, by the breaking of, where
the fragrance is. God damn our grace, that this is how we are fated.

And yet I don't believe I shall repeat him, if for no other reason than,
that I dare not, that I must not (the way my time is quantitative and
must, thus, be turned into space) I must not break, must, somehow,
haul myself up eighty years, god damn these reeds on which men stand.

       Right now, in front of all our eyes, a man child
(sd Bolyai Farkas, on all sides they spring up, to the need of, the
season) is being born — o!
smell the blood.

PART 2

Stamina, that's what isn't, not intelligence. It wasn't only stupidity
the creator damned the race with. It was shortness of life (what Bad
Thing feeds on, knows how to nibble at). And that which we go by
in the running, breath, breath, which can, as the flesh can, give off
the odor of, same flowers.

                    The original sin was simpler: all returns,
we want all returns before one good black night is over, the doctrine
of, what my people
                    (it was the people we used to call the crew) prove,

the whole stink, from the corruption of, are the founders of,
that which gives the lie to, what impugns, exposes
(after christianity, thus
                    the counsel of, the smell of,
                    and of same, the methodology,
                    the fast buck:

                                        kill, kill! he cried,
                                        just to get rid of, just
                                        to avoid

                                        borning, borning, old Bitch Goddess!
                                        you know
                                        the answer

It takes blood, my fellow cits., even to the breaking of
vessels!
          (Vessels!)

PART 3

The ease of (with some of a heart gone, and a little of the lower
intestine, and no one but yourself, no naked white man raised by
brown people to put his hand on, and say, I heal you) the easing of

space. And he says, It sounds easy, only it ain't, as he dressed
himself in doeskin, and went off trading among distant tribes, went
looking for a place where people are still natives, and where human
business is still the business

where, if you can find sleep, see if you can find the ease, see if I
can find you, in your life, moving, as though I were a sea-horse,
because I am, because, god damn it, an olson male is
a double

      multiple, he sd, as a man, or a woman
      is (is a woman?) is
      when they resist, when they let sleep
      that dog with the whitest, sharpest teeth
      the temptation, which didn't get into the biblums,
      that is, into them so far, that is, as I knows them,

        of the brains, which always, always wants
        what it can't have because they ain't

        Answers, I mean,
        which have no smell at all

PART 4

Explaining the magic (where it is, here where he is, he sez, sez time,

"The only trick, the only way you save your thing, or whatever, is
obey, obey, until you've squeezed out of, out of me, out of me who
is yr onlie true enemie. . ."

The sweetest kind of essence, violets
                              is the smell of life.
And I mean serious, like magic is, like
white or black, is
the business we're here for (not here AFTER) i mean (NOW)
the smell of
these flowers
                    And don't expect me to answer,
how come. Nor do I care, even it turns out, as it just might well,
electricals, simply the odor of, from the crackling of,
a wave H-mu, the determinant, human.
                                        Or it doesn't even matter if
they reproduce same. Nature, by way of woman, does it every day.
It is still something, the fragrance, that only those with
the nose for it can smell and
CAN GIVE OFF

                    (Or that line I palmed off on him, as he ate me:
                    "I can be precise,
                      though it is no answer"

                    And why he, after he pushed through so many tribes,
                    had eaten little more than prickly pears,
                    and sucked reeds for water,

why, when he came out—and wasn't it curious, that the point at which
he emerged should have been already called, by the natives, the place
of the heart?—he carefully took the things he had made (despite
Bad Thing, and his botherings) and instead of disposing of them in
so many ways that would occur to you, he merely set them out there
where the rest of the causes of confusion are.
                                        This act of his
is as interesting a proof as anything you shall find, of what we
might call, thinking of the people, and their problems, the other
doctrine, the contrary one, or, what we may simply call, numbers,
numbers seeming now to have a peculiar fascination, like letters, and
other such dry things, as plastics, nipples, and machines—Doctrine
♯2, viz.,

multiple observation at the same instant that others
make less multiple observations, is the difference

(And the which doctrine can also be used to be quite precise about
the difference of this class of worker from other classes of workers,
equally necessary, whatever clothes, or however hy-brid, or what
sort of noses they wear.)

       And, as against 80, 125 years, which,
because the human animal has so shrunk away from created limits,
is no longer the given
                    (thus, the inadequacy of all our work,
compared to the assignment,
and to the equipment given

       Any why we ain't
       spiritchool

         And why there ain't
         antsirs

            And why we damn well have to go
            by the nose
(what nose?)

       Why the whys are, in fact
       (last night, as I sd, he nipped me)
       because they are facts, they are only
       clues:

         It is clews, clews that keep
         sails taut. Drama
         is out of business, tears,
         tears. Ships, ships, it's
         steering now that is, it is
         the biz-i-ness NOW, you
         who care, who can
         endure, it's
         "bring the head 'round, keep
          the wind, citizen!

         (is it not the wind we obey, are
         kept by?

         as good a word as any is
         the SINGLE INTELLIGENCE

PART LAST

At this date of 120 years cut short, I, an olson

in the l'univers concentrationnaire the flesh
(is it not extraordinary that, when a wound
is healing, we call, what it throws off, proud
flesh?) flesh, rose flesh

must also be thrown in.

And because there is no soul (in the old sense),
because there is not (at the old stand, there, now, they sell
gold from teeth,
                    & from burned bones, fertilizers)

amour propre, in the old sense,
won't do.

Now all things (in the furnace of fact, all things)

(no things in the furnace, in the weather-beaten face of

doubt)

now all things (including notions, or whatever
were once validities,
                    all things now stand
(including the likes of you and me, all, all

must be born out of
                    (God knows you know, Old Goddess, &
                       tremendous Mother)

There is birth! there is

all over the place there is

            And if I, in this smother, if I
            smell out one thing sharp,
            or another
           (where his teeth
            have been in me, there—
            even you know, Enemie—
            I speak as modestly as

broken grass which,
under the flood, tries
to breathe, to breathe!

Say I, one blade,
to you, or
whoever:

        it is why there is so much blood
        all over the place

END STORY

Adamo Me . . .

Ride 'em, and, by the ride, down all night, all
apocalypse

   by the, naked, tide, by

beauty, "is most difficult" But
for that reason is, at her tips, not, NOT

to be dum-dummed, you-me, the order of the day is
shall not spread the ends of, with too much teeth, shall
stay in there, without, without, without even

the christ, is a fish, to be caught, especially
where the waves come in, where
(like a wall, they
pour,
   and only with the hands

   (the absolute
    danger of losing, the tow is such, &
    below, the drag
    of the sands)

  can you seize

1

I looked up, and there, on the wall, as though it were on a mesa
and we walking across (or was it others, after us) there
set in clay like a demonstration, vertebra, only vertebra, only
the spines
of what once was.

If the air is wrong, or it is not sand, their houses . . .

Water, water, always water up & over testing, testing, time,
And the little red spot glows, And it is—look! my grandchild,
who is on

       I, merely, bridge, music
       defunctive (he who was I, or
       is it, you?

              "For you," she wrote, "when I am not",
              (coyly, almost, you might say.)

2

When, still, the sea pours in (still
wall) . . . Afterwards,
they sought the sun to dry off, and,

in the hollows of a sand–hill, the flesh
tastes so good they
roll over . . .

Suddenly we stumbled, and, as I sd, I looked down,
and there before my very eyes I was

       (articulated sea-serpent, or the wood
        hewn from that tree which grew up
        where they planted with him who first died
        the seed which the angel had thrust
        into his son's hand that day,
        when the light was coming up, he
        waned
            And they all standing around, his sons & daughters,
      in what astonishment, the morning should bring
      such a new thing!

       Or as small as that extinct bird
       (it was not a bird, it had
       fingers), and though it was not sand,
       it was wind which they sieved,

3

"I can be caught too, preserved,
sd Mme. B.,
for though I am difficult, it is not, for that reason, to be allowed,

you are not to be allowed, Mister B., in the clutch it is not the time
to be called OUT

        Or, for that matter, to cry out, either.

It is too much (too much, musicians say, when, say, a stick), or a
crowd, when you have runners, when you are your own men, when you
have any of us on your hands!

The law, (in her arms we lie), the law
injunctive, hit! hit!
              or
it doesn't matter whether they find you, or yr house, or
even a child, a grandchild, your wife, her handmaiden, or
as they so carefully pan each shovelfull, even yr possessions,
the bones of,
across their knees,
yr dog

    Man built daringly
    by water, there stayed
    because there were always those
    who found other live beings more interesting than

    nature, that is, that what city folk call nature,
    trees, fields, or
    clucking hens

    The riddle is (beside femininity, that is)
    that of which beauty is only the most interesting expression, why
    we persist, why we remain, even in the face of, curious,
    even before the example of

    He dissolved, the second dissolved
    (after some certain punishment, the which
    increaseth, yet, that it doth, does not call for
    such crying out), I dissolve,
    a like scatter of bone, or
    even merely sand,
                And not even shining
    like the neighboring quartz

    actually disappeared, because water
    trickles, or is shaken, or even roars
    over

The news of the day is: 4
were swept down, 4 clung
when the silly glistening powerful match-box of a boat
missed the free-way to the lock and went
swirling over the mill-race, the sluice,
                                        and off, crack,
down the water like fish-eggs or unborn bees
                                        4

were saved, the percentage
a happy one, most
unusual

                        II

The difficulty remains.
But not that it is locked in the mind past all remonstrance,
not at all.

Though this is also true: example,
that they rolled over, that the rose of their flesh shone
where the drops still had not dried in the sun, that, together,
they made a four-legged beast, and, from its making, locked

that from that day they carried away remembrance . . .

                                        none of this, nothing
shows, when, in the sand, you come up on a
dispersed bone,
                but this is (this bone) still (still) no reason
there is none, in this air, there is no reason for
knuckling under, for,

out of difficulty allowing for, submitting to, you, me, all

no reason for

the bribe of

                both beauty AND
                eternity

                the drama OR
                the mashing

                the celebrating OR
                the thrashing

an easy standing OR
a posture

the roaring AND
the epilogue

no reason FOR

both beauty AND
eternity

when, as in each case, an OUT is an OUT!

[Conc.]

That it glows,
that you do,
that you are,
when the flesh is
a rose

That is shine,
that you do, that you'll make,
when the mind is
all glistening

That out of the pouring,
in which you, too, (two, or all
may drown) you, you
shall stand in, shall
in the loud roaring

   (as they lay, in that roaring, they
    took up fire from where fire came,
                                    why
    in their eyes, in her eyes, in his sons' eyes
    there was such bewilderment, such
    discovery, why, it could be, the difficulty, why
    he could be put out!)

Well, still, is there anything,
is there anything you and I shall do more than,
than (the difficulty) be that rose, be
what shining monstrance that we may, be
any more than a hand, a flesh, a force
and stand there in that crashing
water?

And is there anything
(beauty notwithstanding)
more difficult?

END

This

mexico)   could not
have guessed: wood, a
bowl of gray wood, of
an afternoon, already
shadowed (4
pm: very fast, high, sharp
rockets, a crazy trumpet
of a band, few
people, sloppy
cowboys picadors matadors bulls

               but out there, on that dirt, in front, directly
               before your eyes, more, yr existence:
death, the
possibility of same, the certitude
right there in front of yr
eyes, god damn yr
eyes
this bull and this man (these men) can
kill
one another

What one knows
put out, & quietly out, put out right exactly I mean OUT
in front of all eyes, including
     the bull's, who runs out so
         lightly, with such
             declaration of
                 his presence

     the man, so
       careful, such
          preparations (the bull only about to find out), the man
            so clothed, such tools, and
               running back to

                     so ludicrously the
barricade, the bull, too, smelling
the wood, where an opening is, how
to get out of

                                    Whoever
conceived this action, this
thing, this
instant declaration of that which you know is all
that constitutes both what you are and what is going on at all time
as of you or anyone since and as long as whatever
it is that it is, is

        this
        bullfight:

the bull so much not
animal (as the word
is) his
experience so very clear, there, his
bewilderment, tries; angers (no
fear, mere increasing sense from confrontation that
he is
involved

the men (the man) so much more
animal, so
aware, their
courage (fear) so
very clear, so very much the reason why
we too are
involved, why
we, here,

            ((the man, down in that dirt, so much
            a scampering, so much (advancing) a
            sort of picked bantam))

those horns

that voice repeating "to-ro" "to-ro" "to-ro"

those words, wooing

that head, the plain danger of

you

have been

asked

Issue, Mood

                                        still go funny, in the face of
                                        him on money
crazy, straight   like
all-right,   people say, right in the face of
mad   (prat): not chuman not chuman not
                                        hoomin

butchart   butchart   del mar   gesell
        del mar   butchart
                gesell   del mar And the Big

                                        Shot sd
                                                ((I'd
                                        ask the same question (face to) to-
                                        day))
                                                in an-
HE SD: swer (wot
            NAIVE   abt this stamp-tax, this
                                        carrying charge you
                                         & yr dollar
                                         bill)

                                        O BOY, if that don't put
                                        me *on!*
                                                (And the same B.S.,
                                        now?
                                        hamburg, once thru the grinder red, done in, his
                                        so-fist-ik-kashun!)

                                        who dare impugn
                                        another's innocence
By inversal ONLY,   (the inversal, EP to BS,
the   pointed
proposition: this way: white (once through the wringer)
                                        So much else than innocence
                                        being used, being
            NO   thrust on you, IMPOSING (ex., "so that,
                                        when you have yr hands on any BUGGAH"

                    CAN HE?
"Do not,   IS HE,
 "be a Senator,   ABLE
    in yr country, MR.
Poet-Economist   (I think not)

The poles are: HARD METAL vs.
                    NATIONAL DEBT. Now,
I'm a newt dealer, myself, asking,
after so long is it not remarkable
that the creature (even taken out of stone)
breathes.
                    Comes
the revolution, does
this laborer lose
this labor of
his arm?   Or this Lake,

Maracaibo, its
oil?

Either way, it seems to me, he or him, both
Does it not come to, The tidy
fear chaos.

Not to woo it, but,
who's wrong, what's   ...
society.
          and who
be thee? be thee
one of the Innocents?

You see, I take it
there are some certain other premises.
Or, better, some certain other isolated facts
(not worked for, Horatio!) quote:
                                    "the art
of collecting   rising thence by a process of
& arranging,   induction to
          a mass of

              OH YES
reform
          O reform it
          altogether!

                    the habit
to look to society to make it
new.
            bah.
                    (who
cannot honestly make it
stick.)

            Equity?
With the hills?

                    Hills,
                    Sirrah?

Letter for Melville 1951

written to be read AWAY FROM the Melville Society's "One Hundreth Birthday Party" for MOBY DICK at Williams College, Labor Day Weekend, Sept. 2–4, 1951

MY DEAR—:

I do thank you, that we hear from you, but the Melville Society invitation came in the same mail with your news of this thing, and do you for a moment think, who have known me 17 years, that I would come near, that I would have anything to do with their business other than to expose it for the promotion it is, than to do my best to make clear who these creatures are who take on themselves to celebrate a spotless book a wicked man once made?

that I find anywhere in my being any excuse for this abomination, for the false & dirty thing which it is—nothing more than a bunch of commercial travellers from the several colleges? Note this incredible copy: "Those who are planning to take part in the English Institute of Columbia University on September 5–8 will find it convenient to attend both conferences"! Can anything be clearer, as to how Melville is being used? And all the other vulgarities of ease and come-on: how pretty the trees are this time of year, how nice of Williams College to take our fifteen bucks, how you won't run over anyone, the conference is so planned—o no let's not run over anyone but him, and just exactly here in the Berkshire hills where he outwrote himself, just where he—when we go together in the sight-seeing bus—where—the house will be open, it has been arranged—he was very clean with his knife, the arrowhead of his attention having struck, there we'll be able to forget he fell in a rut in that very road and had, thereafter, a most bad crick in his back

o these things we can—we must—not speak of, we must avoid *all* of the traffic except the meals, the sessions, the other points, of interest

for there are most important things to be taken care of: you see, each of us has families (maybe we have as many children as he did) and if we don't or we have only a wife because we really prefer boys, in any case, no matter what the circumstances which we will not mention in the speeches (you know that sort of thing we can only talk about in the halls, outside the meetings, or, at table, out of the corners of our mouths—you might say, out of

a crack in the grave where a certain sort of barbed ivy has broken in
over the years it has lain and multiplied flat on the rather silly stone
others took some care in placing over the remains—we cannot forget,
even for this instant, that, in order, too, that we can think that we
ourselves are of some present importance, we *have* to—I know, we
really would prefer to be free, *but*—we do have to have an income,
so, you see, you must excuse us if we scratch each other's backs with
a dead man's hand

for after all, who but us, who but us has had the niceness to organize
ourselves in his name, who, outside us, is remembering that this man
a year ago one hundred years ago (you see, we *are* very accurate about
our celebration, know such things as dates) was, just where we are
gathering just ahead of labor day (walked coldly in a cold & narrow
hall by one window of that hall to the north, into a room, a very
small room also with one window to the same white north) to avoid
the traffic who is, but us, provided with dormitories and catering
services?

> Timed in such a way to avoid him, to see
> he gets a lot of lip (who hung in a huge jaw)
> and no service at all (none of this chicken, he
> who is beyond that sort of recall, beyond
> any modern highway (which would have saved him
> from sciatica? well, that
> we cannot do for him but we can
> we now know so much, we can make clear
> how he erred, how, in other ways
> —we have made such studies and
> we permit ourselves to think—they
> allow us to tell each other how wise
> he was

He was. Few flying fish
no dolphins and in that glassy sea
two very silly whales throwing
that spout of theirs you might call sibylline
it disappears so fast, why
this year a hundred years ago he
had moved on, was offering
to such as these
a rural bowl of milk, subtitled
the ambiguities

       July
above Sigsbee deep,
the *Lucero del Alba,*

500 tons, 200,000 board feet
of mahogany, the Captain
25, part Negro, part American Indian and perhaps
a little of a certain Cereno, by name
Orestes Camargo
                    Herman Melville
looked up again at the weather, noted
that landlessness   And it was not so much truth
as he had thought, even though the ratlines
could still take his weight (185, eyes
blue, hair auburn, a muscular man knowing
that knowledge
is only what makes a ship shape, takes care
of the precision of the crossed sign, the feather
and the anchor, the thing
which is not the head but is
where they cross, the edge
the moving edge of force, the wed
of sea and sky (or land & sky), the Egyptian
the American backwards

                         (The stern, at evening,
                         a place for conversation, to drop paper boats, to ask
                         why clouds are painters' business, why now he
                         would not write *Moby-Dick*)

Was writing
Pierre: the world
had moved on, in that hallway, moved
north north east, had moved him

                              O such fools
                              neither of virtue nor of truth
                              to associate with
                                              to sit to table by
                         as once before you, and Harry, and I
                         the same table the same Broadhall saw
                         water raised by another such to tell us
                         this beast hauled up out of great water was
                         society!
                                   this Harvard and this Yale
                         as Ossa on Pelion (or,
                         as one less than he but
                         by that lessness still
                         a very great man, said
                         of another—who never learned a thing
                         from Melville—worth
                         "five Oxfords on ten thousand Cambridges"!

o that these fellow diners of your might know
that poets move very fast, that it is true
it is very wise to stay the hell out of
such traffic, of such labor
which knows no weekend

Please to carry my damnations to each of them
as they sit upon their arse-bones variously
however differently padded, or switching

                         to say please, to them
(whom I would not please any more than he will: he is flying
for the weekend, from Pensacola, where,
any moment, he will dock

please say some very simple things, ask them
to be accurate:
ask one to tell you
what it was like to be a Congregational minister's son Midwest
how hard it was for a boy who liked a read to have to pitch, instead,
hay; and how, now that he has published books, now that he has done that
(even though his edition of this here celebrated man's verse
whom we thought we came here to talk about
has so many carelessnesses in it that, as of this date,
it is quite necessary to do it over)
let him tell you, that no matter how difficult it is
to work in an apartment in a bedroom in a very big city
because the kids are bothersome and have to be locked out, and the wife
is only too good, yet, he did republish enough of this other man
to now have a different professional title, a better salary
and though he wishes he were at Harvard or a Whale,
he is, isn't he, if he is quite accurate, much more liked
by his president?

There'll be main speeches, and one
will do the same thing that other did that other time, tell you
(as he did then who has, since, lost a son in war, society
is such a shambles, such a beast, and altogether not
that white whale), this new one, this new book-maker
will talk about democracy, has such a nose
is so imbued with progress he will classify
the various modes of same (what,
because it was the '30's, and hope was larger, that other
gave us in a broader view) but press him, ask him
is it not true you have, instead, made all this make your way
into several little magazines however old they are?

<pre>   (How much light
            the black & white man threw—Orestes!—on
            democracy!)

            as, if you were on the floor that night, you could see
            just what are the differences of the hidden rears
            of each of your fellow celebrators
</pre>

Myself, I'd like to extricate you who have the blood of him, and another
who loves him as a doctor knows
a family doctor, how
his mother stayed inside him, how
the compact came out hate, and what
this kept him from, despite
how far he travelled

<pre>   (The match-box, with a match for mast,
                              goes backward gaily, bumping
                              along the wake)
</pre>

What they'll forget—they'll smother you—is
there is only one society, there is no other than
how many we do not know, where
and why they read a book, and that
the reading of a book can save a life, they
do not come to banquets, and Nathaniel Hawthorne
whom Herman Melville loved
will not come, nor Raymond Weaver
who loved them both because they loved each other.

You have the right to be there
because you loved an old man's walk
and took a little attic box, and books.
And there is he, the doctor, whom I love
and by his presence side by side with you
will speak for Melville and myself, he
who was himself saved, who
because, in the middle of the Atlantic,
an appendectomy was called for, read
a sea story once, and since
has gone by the pole-star, a scalpel overside
for rudder, has moved on from Calypso, huge
in the despatch of
the quick-silver god

Yet I wish so very much that neither of you mixed
(as Leyda hasn't) in this middle place, in such salad
as these caterers will serve!

For you will have to hear one very bright man speak, so bright
he'll sound so good that every one of you will think
he knows whereof he speaks, he'll say such forward things, he'll tag
the deific principle in nature, the heroic
principle in man, he'll spell
what you who do not have such time to read as he
such definitions so denotatively clear you'll think you'll understand
(discourse is such a lie) that Herman Melville
was no professional, could not accomplish
such mentality and so, as amateur (as this clear neuter will make clear)
was anguished all his life in struggle, not with himself, he'll say,
no, not with when
shall i eat my lunch Elizabeth has set outside the door so quiet
it was not even a mouse, my prose today
is likewise, the cows, what a damned nuisance they also are, why
do i continue to extend my language horizontally when
i damn well know what is
a water-spout

No, he'll skillfully confuse you, he knows such words
as mythic, such adjectives that fall so easily you'll think it's true
Melville was a risky but creative mingling
                         (how they put words on, that this lad was so
who stowed himself with roaches and a blue-shining corpse at age 16: "Hey!
Jackson!"

                    the diced bones—now this too, he
                    who is also of the one society
                    who likewise lifted altars
                    too high (a typewriter
                    in a tree) and spilled himself
                    into the honey-head, died
                    the blond ant
                    so pleasantly

                              as though he did not want to woo
                              to chance a Bronx grave, preferred
                              to choose his own headland

All these that you will sit with—"a mingling," he will drone on,
"of the fortunate and the injurious"

And only you, and Harry (who knows)
will not be envious, will know
that he knows not one thing
this brightest of these mischievous men
who does not know that it is not the point
either of the hook or the plume which lies
cut on this brave man's grave
—on all of us—
but that where they cross is motion,
where they constantly moving cross anew, cut
this new instant open—as he is who
is this weekend in his old place
presumed on

                              I tell you,

he'll look on you all with an eye you have the color of.

He'll not say a word because he need not, he said so many.

The Laughing Ones

they
are the light-hearted races,
enjoy nothing so much, obviously,
as the cracking of skulls (Tyro's fields
were covered with 'em

their mortality
is altogether pervasive, these
chillun of the sun

the earth (the Others
call it darkling)
they flee. Persephone
is never of their making,
Demeter neither. Women
are delights, things to run with, equals
—small game they slay

it is true: the sun breeds slayers, makers of spring
and slayers. (There it is: Celts,
light, light, thin with it
And only in love with the dark,
which they never know. How
can they? their blood
does not go down, it
races out! And they like it—
out! They only remember
what space has had her arms around.

You dark men root in woman as a cave, they
(the splinters)
want to dance, only to dance
& slay. They
are without suspicion, stupid, gay, think
the world is a banquet leading not to conversation but
a scrap!

O

what shall men do with these empty-heads
before they destroy us? what shall you do, you
who favor the beat
not the color of
blood?

what shall we do to bring them down, the laughing ones
who do not have beautiful teeth?

He, who in his abandoned infancy,
spoke of Jesus, Caesar, those who beg
and Hell

Crossed-over dreams, or infertile
crusades, made such
by the filth and lumber
of the present leadership, o!
may they be sucked up
by their own orange cloud, their own
displaced sea, they
who can teach nothing of vice
or of a death without regrets, nothing
of a life so lived

This one, awake
(ending his life in a sort of continuing dream)
spoke of strange things sweetly
(as he had made verse sweet in his time)
with a voice which would have raised me
had my own heart not been squeezed
this narrow.

The doctors said
they did not understand

The Dry Ode

It pusheth us out before it, out, and to the side.
    Gray stalks in a green field.
    Young corn in clay. And the heart,
    a seed. And the head,
    how heavy is the yield?

The crops are grass, mainly.

We make shift to do, holding down.
    Corn is as corn was. And now
    the soil is gray, the flower
    alfalfa, green, it is, is green
    again

Rotate (like they say) the clover, the grain. Go round
    the field-stone
    (or the brick-walled center, grave, whichever
    local
    to the native
    ground

For in the shade are rocks, some mustard plant, the sun
diffuse

The movement is, generally as, as weather
comes from the west.

La Préface

The dead in via
         in vita nuova
                in the way
You shall lament who know they are as tender as the horse is.
You, do not you speak who know not.

      "I will die about April 1st . . ." going off
      "I weigh, I think, 80 lbs . . ." scratch
      "My name is NO RACE"   address
      Buchenwald   new Altamira cave
      With a nail they drew the object of the hunt.

Put war away with time, come into space.
It was May, precise date, 1940. I had air my lungs could breathe.
He talked, via stones   a stick   sea rock   a hand of earth.
It is now, precise, repeat. I talk of Bigmans organs
he, look, the lines! are polytopes.
And among the DPs—deathhead
                  at the apex
                      of the pyramid.

Birth in the house is the One of Sticks, cunnus in the crotch.
Draw it thus: (   ) 1910 (
It is not obscure. We are the new born, and there are no flowers.
Document means there are no flowers
                  and no parenthesis.

It is the radical, the root, he and I, two bodies
We put our hands to these dead.

The closed parenthesis reads: the dead bury the dead,
                  and it is not very interesting.
Open, the figure stands at the door, horror his
and gone, possessed, o new Osiris, Odysseus ship.
He put the body there as well as they did whom he killed.

Mark that arm. It is no longer gun.
We are born not of the buried but these unburied dead
crossed stick, wire-led, Blake Underground

The Babe
      the Howling Babe

The Kingfishers

1

What does not change / is the will to change

He woke, fully clothed, in his bed. He
remembered only one thing, the birds, how
when he came in, he had gone around the rooms
and got them back in their cage, the green one first,
she with the bad leg, and then the blue,
the one they had hoped was a male

Otherwise? Yes, Fernand, who had talked lispingly of Albers & Angkor Vat.
He had left the party without a word. How he got up, got into his coat,
I do not know. When I saw him, he was at the door, but it did not matter,
he was already sliding along the wall of the night, losing himself
in some crack of the ruins. That it should have been he who said, "The kingfishers!
who cares
for their feathers
now?"

His last words had been, "The pool is slime." Suddenly everyone,
ceasing their talk, sat in a row around him, watched
they did not so much hear, or pay attention, they
wondered, looked at each other, smirked, but listened,
he repeated and repeated, could not go beyond his thought
"The pool   the kingfishers' feathers were wealth   why
did the export stop?"

It was then he left

2

I thought of the E on the stone, and of what Mao said
la lumiere"
                    but the kingfisher
de l'aurore"
                    but the kingfisher flew west

est devant nous!
                  he got the color of his breast
                  from the heat of the setting sun!

The features are, the feebleness of the feet (syndactylism of the 3rd & 4th digit)
the bill, serrated, sometimes a pronounced beak, the wings
where the color is, short and round, the tail
inconspicuous.

But not these things were the factors. Not the birds.
The legends are
legends. Dead, hung up indoors, the kingfisher
will not indicate a favoring wind,
or avert the thunderbolt. Nor, by its nesting,
still the waters, with the new year, for seven days.
It is true, it does nest with the opening year, but not on the waters.
It nests at the end of a tunnel bored by itself in a bank. There,
six or eight white and translucent eggs are laid, on fishbones
not on bare clay, on bones thrown up in pellets by the birds.

                  On these rejectamenta
(as they accumulate they form a cup-shaped structure) the young are born.
And, as they are fed and grow, this nest of excrement and decayed fish becomes
                  a dripping, fetid mass

Mao concluded:
                nous devons
                        nous lever
                                et agir!

3

When the attentions change / the jungle
 leaps in
        even the stones are split
                they rive

Or,
enter
that other conqueror we more naturally recognize
he so resembles ourselves

But the E
cut so rudely on the oldest stone
sounded otherwise,
was differently heard

as, in another time, were treasures used:

(and, later, much later, a fine ear thought
 a scarlet coat)

        "of green feathers feet, beaks and eyes
          of gold

        "animals likewise,
          resembling snails

        "a large wheel, gold, with figures of unknown four-foots,
          and worked with tufts of leaves, weight
          3800 ounces

        "last, two birds, of thread and freatherwork, the quills
          gold, the feet
          gold, the two birds perched on two reeds
          gold, the reeds arising from two embroidered mounds,
          one yellow, the other
          white.

        "And from each reed hung
          seven feathered tassels.

In this instance, the priests
(in dark cotton robes, and dirty,
their dishevelled hair matted with blood, and flowing wildly
over their shoulders)
rush in among the people, calling on them
to protect their gods

And all now is war
where so lately there was peace,
and the sweet brotherhood, the use
of tilled fields.

4

Not one death but many,
not accumulation but change, the feed-back proves, the feed-back is
the law

        Into the same river no man steps twice
        When fire dies air dies
        No one remains, nor is, one

Around an appearance, one common model, we grow up
many. Else how is it,
if we remain the same,
we take pleasure now
in what we did not take pleasure before? love
contrary objects? admire and/or find fault? use
other words, feel other passions, have
nor figure, appearance, disposition, tissue
the same?
            To be in different states without a change
            is not a possibility

We can be precise. The factors are
in the animal and/or the machine the factors are
communication and/or control, both involve
the message. And what is the message? The message is
a discrete or continuous sequence of measurable events distributed in time

is the birth of air, is
the birth of water, is
a state between
the origin and
the end, between
birth and the beginning of
another fetid nest

is change, presents
no more than itself

And the too strong grasping of it,
when it is pressed together and condensed,
loses it

This very thing you are

                    II

            They buried their dead in a sitting posture
            serpent   cane   razor   ray of the sun

            And she sprinkled water on the head of the child, crying
            "Cioa-coatl! Cioa-coatl!"
            with her face to the west

            Where the bones are found, in each personal heap
            with what each enjoyed, there is always
            the Mongolian louse

The light is in the east. Yes. And we must rise, act. Yet
in the west, despite the apparent darkness (the whiteness
which covers all), if you look, if you can bear, if you can, long enough

        as long as it was necessary for him, my guide
        to look into the yellow of that longest-lasting rose

so you must, and, in that whiteness, into that face, with what candor, look

and considering the dryness of the place
      the long absence of an adequate race

        (of the two who first came, each a conquistador, one healed, the other
        tore the eastern idols down, toppled
        the temple walls, which, says the excuser
        were black from human gore)

hear
hear, where the dry blood talks
      where the old appetite walks

                        la piu saporita et migliore
                        che si possa truovar al mondo

where it hides, look
in the eye how it runs
in the flesh / chalk

        but under these petals
        in the emptiness
        regard the light, contemplate
        the flower

whence it arose

        with what violence benevolence is bought
        what cost in gesture justice brings
        what wrongs domestic rights involve
        what stalks
        this silence

        what pudor pejorocracy affronts
        how awe, night-rest and neighborhood can rot
        what breeds where dirtiness is law
        what crawls
        below

III

I am no Greek, hath not th'advantage.
And of course, no Roman:
he can take no risk that matters,
the risk of beauty least of all.

But I have my kin, if for no other reason than
(as he said, next of kin) I commit myself, and,
given my freedom, I'd be a cad
if I didn't. Which is most true.

It works out this way, despite the disadvantage.
I offer, in explanation, a quote:
si j'ai du goût, ce n'est guères
que pour la terre et les pierres.

Despite the discrepancy (an ocean   courage   age)
this is also true: if I have any taste
it is only because I have interested myself
in what was slain in the sun

    I pose you your question:

shall you uncover honey / where maggots are?

    I hunt among stones

ABCs

The word forms
on the left: you must
stand in line. Speech
is as swift as synapse
but the acquisition of same
is as long
as I am old

    r a t   on the first floor landing of the three-decker
                 (grey)

   b l a c k   eat a peck of storage batteries 'fore
                 I die

c a b b a g e   my friend Cabbage, with whom to bake potatoes up
                 Fisher's Hill

   r u s t   in the bed of Beaver Brook—from the junk in it
                 And the iris ("flags," we called 'em)
                 And the turtle I was surprised by

up to last night's dream, the long brown body pleased
I kissed her buttock curve

Interiors,
and their registration

Words, form
but the extension of
content

Style, est verbum

The word
is image, and the reverend reverse is
Eliot

Pound
is verse

ABCs (2)

what we do not know of ourselves
of who they are who lie
coiled or unflown
in the marrow of the bone

    one sd:

        of rhythm is image
        of image is knowing
        of knowing there is
        a construct

or to find in a night who it is dwells in that wood where shapes hide
who is this woman or this man whose face we give a name to, whose shoulder
we bite, what landscape
figures ride small horses over, what bloody stumps
these dogs have, how they tear the golden cloak

                        And the boat,
how he swerves it to avoid the yelping rocks
where the tidal river rushes

ABCs (3—for Rimbaud)

NEWS (o the latest)
& mu-sick, mu-sick—music
worse than war, worse
than peace, & they both dead
And the people's faces
like boils

Who pleas for the heart, for the return of, into the work of,
say, the running of
a street car?

    Or shall it be rain,
    on a tent   or grass   or birds
    on a wire (5, count 'em, now 3
    on two—or does it come to 1
    on 1? Is it
    Metechevsky?
              We call it
              trillings, cleanings,
              we who want scourings

    Or the watching of, the Passaic of
    orange peels? Cats
    win in urbe, NOT
    usura   or those queer long white (like finger bandages
    balloons? The dyes
    of realism? (Cats,
    & industry, not even
    violence

              Why not the brutal, head on?
              Fruits? beauty? to want it
              so hard? Who
              can beat that life
              into form, who
              is so hopeful—who
              has mislead us?

To have what back? Is it any more than
a matter of
syllables?

Yes, mouths bit
empty air

                     They bit. What
                     do they bite,
                     now? what we needed most
                     was something the extension of
                     claritas: what do we have
                     to report?

(until then, do you hear,
 you whose ears bulge,
 sered eyes
 are at rest)

There was a Youth
whose Name was Thomas Granger

1

From the beginning, SIN
and the reason, note, known from the start

says Mr. bradford: As it is with waters when
their streames are stopped or damed up, wickednes
(Morton, Morton, Morton)
here by strict laws as in no place more,
or so much, that I have known or heard of,
and yᵉ same more nerly looked unto
(Tom Granger)
so, as it cannot rune in a comone road of liberty
as it would, and is inclined,
it searches every wher (everywhere)
and breaks out wher it getts vente, says he

Rest, Tom, in your pit where they put you
a great & large pitte digged of purposs for them
of Duxbery, servant, being aboute 16. or 17. years of age
his father & mother living at the time at Sityate

espetially drunkennes & unclainnes
incontinencie betweene persons unmaried
but some maried persons allso
And that which is worse
(things fearfull to name)

HAVE BROAK FORTH OFTENER THAN ONCE
IN THIS LAND

2

indicated for yᵉ same) with
a mare, a cowe, tow goats, five sheep, 2. calves
and a turkey (Plymouth Plantation)

Now follows yᵉ ministers answers

3

Mr Charles Channcys   a reverend, godly, very larned man
who shortly thereafter, due to a difference aboute baptising
he holding it ought only to be by diping
that sprinkling was unlawful, removed him selfe
to the same Sityate, a minister to ye church ther

in this case proved, by reference to ye judicials of Moyses
& see: Luther, Calvin, Hen: Bulin:. Theo: Beza. Zanch:
what greevous sin in ye sight of God,
by ye instigation of burning lusts, set on fire of hell,
to proceede to contactum & fricationem ad emissionem seminis,
          &c.,
& yt contra naturam, or to attempt ye grosse acts of

4

Mr Bradford: I forbear perticulers.
And accordingly he was cast by ye jury,
and condemned.

              It being demanded of him
the youth confessed he had it of another
who had long used it in old England,
and they kept catle togeather.

And after executed about ye 8. of Septr, 1642.
              A very sade spectakle it was; for first the mare,
and then ye cowe, and ye rest of ye lesser catle,
were kild before his face, according to ye law
Levit: 20.15.

and then he him selfe

                    and no use made of any part of them

Siena

Awkwardness, the grace
the absence of the suave

At once/ a boy walks out of his father's house
a field planted to angles & infinity goes off
/ and above/ the boy enters the desert to meet
the Christ
          He meets the Christ

Lazarus is raised by a glance

Two men cast a net / a third stands on the shore
The sea is grass, and the fish,
as large as the boat, are
flowers. The boat is
as a child carves
wood. He on the shore is
the Christ
          The Christ is a fish

Nicholas hovers over the city walls

Wolves came in close in those days
or tore the farmer's child. But shall we say
miracles are not necessary now
to stop marauders?
Claire, Francis be
our protection
          at sea/ before the sultan/ death

From the trough of the wave where only our heads show
the ship a postcard sunk in hillocks thru which swim
a man wrenched round to point at him who like a haloed stump
raises his hand above us
          we   who are awkward   ask

Other Than

cold
    cold
        on the bold

shore, as the rock
falleth the water
stands: beware

of permanence, you who would run in, who, in yr thin shallops, think
to make the land

the season
        is forever
                cold,
and the reason the rock

(if you can call the mind

Or is it from water

that images

come?

And the boldness
never to be ice, never
to stand, never to go other than does
the slow & antient
heart: to change

is the expectation

            we previous immigrants
            tell you

At Yorktown

1
At Yorktown the church
at Yorktown the dead
at Yorktown the grass
are live

      at York-town the earth
piles itself in shallows,
declares itself, like water,
by pools and mounds

2
At Yorktown the dead
are soil
at Yorktown the church
is marl
at Yorktown the swallows
dive where it is greenest,

            the hollows
are eyes are flowers, the heather,
equally accurate, is hands

      at York-town only the flies
dawdle, like history,
in the sun

3

at Yorktown the earth works
braw
at Yorktown the mortars
of brass, weathered green, of mermaids
for handles, of Latin
for texts, scream
without noise
like a gull

4

At Yorktown the long dead
loosen the earth, heels
sink in, over an abatis
a bird wheels

and time is a shine caught blue
from a martin's
back

The Praises

She who was burned more than half her body skipped out of death

Observing
that there are five solid figures, the Master
(or so Aetius reports, in the *Placita*)
concluded that
the Sphere of the Universe arose from
the dodecahedron

        whence Alexander,
        appearing in a dream to Antiochus,
        showed him
        And on the morrow, the enemy (the Galates)
        ran before it,
        before the sign, that is

1

By Filius Bonaci, his series, rediscovered Pisa 1202, we shall attack,
for it, too, proceeds asymptotically toward the graphic and tangible, the law
now determined to be
phi

        its capital role in the distribution of
        leaves   seeds   branches on a stem (ex.,
        the ripe sun–flower)

        the ratios $\frac{5}{8}$, $\frac{8}{13}$
        in the seed–cones of fir–trees,
        the ratio $\frac{21}{34}$
        in normal daisies

        Pendactylism is general in the animal kingdom.
        But crystals . . . there, pentagonal forms or lattices
        do not, can not appear

So we have it : star and jelly fish, the sea urchin.
And because there is an ideal and constant angle which,
for leaves and branches on a stem, produces
the maximum exposition to light, that light vertical,
fruit blossoms   the briar rose   the passion flower
But lilies   tulips   the hyacinth, like crystals . . .

Here we must stop   And ponder   For nature,
though she is, as you know (so far, that is
as it is allowed to a mortal to know) from all points of view
similar to herself, yet minerals . . .

       o, that's not fair, let
       woman keep her jewels, odd man
       his pleasure of her glow, let
       your lady Nephritite
       pumice her malachite, paint
       her lids green against the light

Sd he:
    to dream takes no effort
       to think is easy
          to act is more difficult
but for a man to act after he has taken thought, this!
is the most difficult thing of all

2

We turn now to Ammonius,
who was present when Nero was,
who is full of delights,
& who smiles quickly

    the epiphanies, he says, in this case are four:
    1st, to such as begin to learn & to inquire,
    the Pythian response,
    with flute

    (2) when part of the truth is glimpsed, the sun
    (a creature of four-fold eyes and heads,
    of a ram   a bull   a snake   the bright-eyed lion)
    This is little, even though the drum
    is added

When a person has got the knowledge, Ammonius
(and he does not mean to be ambiguous)
confers one overwhelming title:
he says a man may then call himself OF THEBES. He may sing

The last, and triumphant mode. I leave, as he leaves it,
untranslated : when men are active, enjoy thought, that is to say
when they talk, they are LESKENOI. They rage

Which is why what is related must remain enigmatic
And why Ammonius excepts, from these epiphanies,
those who are entirely brutish.

Which brings us to what concerns us in the present inquiry.

    Avert, avert, avoid
    pollution, to be clean
    in a dirty time

                O Wheel, aid us
                to get the gurry off

    You would have a sign. Look:
    to fly? a fly can do that;

    to try the moon? a moth
    as well; to walk on water? a straw
    precedes you

                O Wheel! draw
                that truth
                to my house

    Like pa does, not like sis,
    on all detractors, piss, o advertised earth!
    And you, o lady Moon, observe my love,
    whence it arose

    Whence it arose,
    and who it is who sits,
    there at the base of the skull, locked
    in his throne of bone, that mere pea of bone
    where the axes meet, cross-roads of the system
    god, converter, discloser, he will answer,
    will look out, if you will look, look!

3

What has been lost
is the secret of secrecy, is
the value, viz., that the work get done, and quickly,
without the loss of due and profound respect for
the materials

which is not so easy as it sounds, nor
can it permit the dispersion which follows from
too many having too little
knowledge

                         Says Iamblichus:
        by shipwreck, he perished (Hippasus, that is)
        the first to publish (write down, divulge)
        the secret,
        the construction of, from 12 pentagons,
        the sphere

        "Thus was he punished for his impiety"

What is necessary is
containment,
that that which has been found out by work may, by work, be passed on
(without due loss of force)
for use
        USE

"And they took over power, political power, in Gr Greece, including
Sicily, and maintained themselves, even after the Master died, until,
at Metapontum, the mob

"Only Philalaos, and Lysis, did not perish in the fire. Later,
Archytas it was, pupil of Philalaos, who, friend to Plato, initiated him,
and, at Tarentum

4

Which is about what we had to say,
the clues, anyhow

What belongs to art and reason is
                      the knowledge of
                              consequences

L da V, his notebook:

Every natural action obeys by
the straightest possible process

It is the use, it is the use
you make of us, the use
you make of
you!

La Chute

my drum, hollowed out thru the thin slit,
carved from the cedar wood, the base I took
when the tree was felled

o my lute, wrought from the tree's crown

my drum, whose lustiness
was not to be resisted

                      my lute,
from whose pulsations
not one could turn away

                            They
are where the dead are, my drum fell
where the dead are, who
will bring it up, my lute
who will bring it up where it fell in the face of them
where they are, where my lute and drum have fallen?

In Cold Hell, in Thicket

In cold hell, in thicket, how
abstract (as high mind, as not lust, as love is) how
strong (as strut or wing, as polytope, as things are
constellated) how
strung, how cold
can a man stay (can men) confronted
thus?

All things are made bitter, words even
are made to taste like paper, wars get tossed up
like lead soldiers used to be
(in a child's attic) lined up
to be knocked down, as I am,
by firings from a spit-hardened fort, fronted
as we are, here, from where we must go

God, that man, as his acts must, as there is always
a thing he can do, he can raise himself, he raises
on a reed he raises his

Or, if it is me, what
he has to say

1

What has he to say?
In hell it is not easy
to know the traceries, the markings
(the canals, the pits, the mountings by which space
declares herself, arched, as she is, the sister,
awkward stars drawn for teats to pleasure him, the brother
who lies in stasis under her, at ease as any monarch or
a happy man

How shall he who is not happy, who has been so made unclear,
who is no longer privileged to be at ease, who, in this brush, stands
reluctant, imageless, unpleasured, caught in a sort of hell, how
shall he convert this underbrush, how turn this unbidden place
how trace and arch again
the necessary goddess?

2

The branches made against the sky are not of use, are
already done, like snow-flakes, do not, cannot service
him who has to raise   (Who puts this on, this damning of his flesh?)
he can, but how far, how sufficiently far can he raise the thickets of
this wilderness?

How can he change, his question is
these black and silvered knivings, these
awkwardnesses?

How can he make these blood-points into panels, into sides
for a king's, for his own
for a wagon, for a sleigh, for the beak of, the running sides of
a vessel fit for
moving?

How can he make out, he asks,
of this low eye-view,
size?

And archings traced and picked enough to hold
to stay, as she does, as he, the brother, when,
here where the mud is, he is frozen, not daring
where the grass grows, to move his feet from fear
he'll trespass on his own dissolving bones, here
where there is altogether too much remembrance?

3

The question, the fear he raises up himself against
(against the same each act is proffered, under the eyes
each fix, the town of the earth over, is managed) is: Who
am I?

Who am I but by a fix, and another,
a particle, and the congery of particles carefully picked one by another,

as in this thicket, each
smallest branch, plant, fern, root
—roots lie, on the surface, as nerves are laid open—
must now (the bitterness of the taste of her) be
isolated, observed, picked over, measured, raised
as though a word, an accuracy were a pincer!
                                                                        this
is the abstract, this
is the cold doing, this
is the almost impossible

So shall you blame those
who give it up, those who say
it isn't worth the struggle?

                                        (Prayer
Or a death as going over to—shot by yr own forces—to
a greener place?

                                Neither

any longer
usable)

                        By fixes only (not even any more by shamans)
                        can the traceries
                        be brought out

                II

ya, selva oscura, but hell now
is not exterior, is not to be got out of, is
the coat of your own self, the beasts
emblazoned on you   And who
can turn this total thing, invert
and let the ragged sleeves be seen
by any bitch or common character?   Who
can endure it where it is, where the beasts are met,
where yourself is, your beloved is, where she
who is separate from you, is not separate, is not
goddess, is, as your core is,
the making of one hell

                        where she moves off, where she is
                        no longer arch

    (this is why he of whom we speak does not move, why
     he stands so awkward where he is, why
     his feet are held, like some ragged crane's
     off the nearest next ground, even from
     the beauty of the rotting fern his eye
     knows, as he looks down, as,
     in utmost pain if cold can be so called,
     he looks around this battlefield, this
     rotted place where men did die, where boys
     and immigrants have fallen, where nature
     (the years that she's took over)
     does not matter, where

that men killed, do kill, that woman kills
is part, too, of his question

2

That it is simple, what the difference is—
that a man, men, are now their own wood
and thus their own hell and paradise
that they are, in hell or in happiness, merely
something to be wrought, to be shaped, to be carved, for use, for
others

does not in the least lessen his, this unhappy man's
obscurities, his
confrontations

He shall step, he
will shape, he
is already also
moving off

      into the soil, on to his own bones

he will cross

      (there is always a field,
       for the strong there is always
       an alternative)

             But a field
      is not a choice, is
      as dangerous as a prayer, as a death, as any
      misleading, lady

He will cross

      And is bound to enter (as she is)
      a later wilderness.
                Yet
      what he does here, what he raises up
      (he must, the stakes are such

                     this at least
      is a certainty, this
      is a law, is not one of the questions, this
      is what was talked of as
      —what was it called, demand?)

He will do what he now does, as she will, do
carefully, do
without wavering,
without
       as even the branches,
       even in this dark place, the twigs
                      how
       even the brow
of what was once to him a beautiful face

as even the snow-flakes waver in the light's eye

       as even forever wavers (gutters
       in the wind of loss)

       even as he will forever waver

       precise as hell is, precise
       as any words, or wagon,
       can be made

Move Over

Merchants.   of the sea and of finance

(Smash the plate glass window)

The dead face is the true face
of Washington, New York a misery, but north and east
the carpenter obeyed
topography

As a hand addresses itself to the care of plants
and a sense of proportion, the house
is put to the earth

Tho peopled with hants, New England

Move over to let the death-blow in,
the unmanned or the transvest, drest
in beard and will, the capillary

Seven years with the wrong man,
7 yrs of tristus and vibullation.
And I looked up to see a toad. And the boy sd:
"I crushed one, and its blood is green"

Green, is the color of my true love's green
despite
New England is
despite her merchants and her morals

A Round
&
A Canon

1   As, certainly, it is not you who sway
    (Black-eyed Susan) but it is the wind
    has this affection for you

        that this child of mine
                     hangs
    where the arc does not yet know which
    (the swing does not) the moment
    over or back, innocent or wise

    in mid-air

    about to fall either way is such
    a lovely bird of a wild human motion

2   A bird
    knows too much, or it strikes me he knows enough
    to awake to a day to sing a day down

        And when he falls—o
    all saints & recitals, consider
    what a very high heart, what a high heat

              such nerves
    I cannot keep him alive, holding
    him in my hand, winged or pawed, he fell
    from his own world, his own careful context, those
    balances

        Even a spoon
    of the finest honey, or a splint, or,
    tried down his throat like his father,
    the finest worm

Won't do. He dies, his eyes
close upward, the film first, the milky way
of his dying
                    (as the Two who shyly rule
off the north in the night settle, distractedly,
in the sea

                    He ceases to fly or to sing. And no reference
to the twisting of the neck of
the spitting black goose

                                        he dies
as the instant dies, as I die
for an instant listening
to the slightest
error

The Moon is the Number 18

is a monstrance,
the blue dogs bay,
and the son sits,
grieving

is a grinning god, is
the mouth of, is
the dripping moon

while in the tower the cat
preens
and all motion
is a crab

and there is nothing he can do but what they do, watch
the face of waters, and fire

       The blue dogs paw,
       lick the droppings, dew
       or blood, whatever
       results are. And night,
       the crab, rays round
       attentive as the cat to catch
       human sound

       The blue dogs rue,
       as he does, as he would howl, confronting
       the wind which rocks what was her, while prayers
       striate the snow, words blow
       as questions cross fast, fast
       as flames, as flames form, melt
       along any darkness

Birth is an instance as is a host, namely, death

The moon has no air

In the red tower
in that tower where she also sat
in that particular tower where watching & moving are,
there,
there where what triumph there is, is: there
is all substance, all creature
all there is against the dirty moon, against
number, image, sortilege—.

alone with cat & crab,
and sound is, is, his
conjecture

La Torre

The tower is broken, the house
where the head was used to lift,
where awe was
And the hands

> (It is broken!
> And the sounds
> are sweet, the air
> acrid, in the night fear
> is fragrant

>> The end of something has a satisfaction.
>> When the structures go, light
>> comes through

To begin again. Lightning
is an axe, transfer
of force subject to object is
order : destroy!

> To destroy
> is start again, is a factor of
> sun, fire is
> when the sun is out, dowsed

>>> (To cause the jaws to grind
>>> before the nostrils flare
>>> to let breath in

Stand clear! Here
it comes down and with it the heart has
what was, what was
we do lament

> Let him who knows not how to pray
> go to sea

>> Where there are no walls
>> there are no laws, forms, sounds, odors
>> to grab hold of

Let the tower fall!
Where space is born
man has a beach to ground on

> We have taken too little note of this:
> the sound of a hammer on a nail can be as clear as
> the blood a knife can make spurt from a round taut belly

2

In the laden air
we are no longer cold.
Birds spring up, and on the fragrant sea
rafts come toward us lashed of wreckage and young tree.
They bring the quarried stuff we need to try this new-found strength.
It will take new stone, new tufa, to finish off this rising tower.

For Sappho, Back

I

With a dry eye, she
saw things out of the corner of,
with a bold
she looked on any man,
with a shy eye

With a cold eye, with her eye she looked on, she looked out, she
who was not so different as you might imagine from,
who had, as nature had, an eye to look upon her makings, to,
in her womb, know
how red, and because it is red, how
handsome blood is, how, because it is unseen, how
because it goes about its business as she does,
as nature's things have that way of doing, as
in the delight of her eye she
creates constants
                    And, in the thickness of her blood, some
variants

II

As blood is, as flesh can be
is she, self-housed, and moving
moving in impeccability to be
clear, clear! to be
as, what is rhythm but
her limpidity?
                She
who is as certain as the morning is
when it arises, when it is spring, when, from wetness comes its brightness
as fresh as this beloved's fingers, lips
each new time she new turns herself to
tendernesses, she
turns her most objective, scrupulous attention, her own
self-causing
            each time it is,
            as is the morning, is
            the morning night and revelation of her
            nakednesses, new
            forever new, as fresh as is the scruple of her eye, the accurate
            kiss

III

If you would know what woman is, what
strength the reed of man unknows, forever
cannot know, look, look! in these eyes, look
as she passes, on this moving thing, which moves
as grass blade by grass blade moves, as
syllable does throw light on fellow syllable, as,
in this rare creature, each hidden, each moving thing
is light to its known, unknown brother,
as objects stand one by one by another, so
is this universe, this flow, this woman, these eyes
are sign

IV

The intimate, the intricate, what shall perplex, forever
is a matter, is it not, not of confusions to be studied and made literal,
but of a dry dance by which, as shoots one day make leaves, as
the earth's crust, when ice draws back, wrings mountains
from itself, makes valleys in whose palms
root-eating fisher folk spring up—
by such a dance, in which the dancer contradicts
the waste and easy gesture, contains
the heave within,
within, because the human is so light a structure, within
a finger, say, or there
within the gentlest swaying of
                              (of your true hips)

In such containment
                    And in search for that which is the shoot, the thrust
of what you are
            (of what you were so delicately born)
                                        of what fruits
of your own making you are
                        the hidden constance of which all the rest
is awkward variation

                    this! this
                    is what gives beauty to her eye, inhabitation
                    to her tender-taken bones, is what illumines
                    all her skin with satin glow
                    when love blows over, turning
                    as the leaf turns in the wind
                    and, with that shock of recognition, shows
                    its other side, the joy, the sort of terror of

                    a dancer going off

The Ring of

it was the west wind caught her up, as
she rose
from the genital
wave, and bore her from the delicate
foam, home
to her isle

and those lovers
of the difficult, the hours
of the golden day welcomed her, clad her, were
as though they had made her, were wild
to bring this new thing born
of the ring of the sea pink
& naked, this girl, brought her
to the face of the gods, violets
in her hair

Beauty, and she
said no to zeus & them all, all were not or
was it she chose the ugliest
to bed with, or was it straight
and to expiate the nature of beauty, was it?

knowing hours, anyway,
she did not stay long, or the lame
was only one part, & the handsome
mars had her And the child
had that name, the arrow of
as the flight of, the move of
his mother who adorneth

with myrtle the dolphin and words
they rise, they do who
are born of like
elements

An Ode on Nativity

I

All cries rise, & the three of us
observe how fast Orion
marks midnight
at the climax
of the sky

    while the boat of the moon settles
as red in the southwest
as the orb of her was, for this boy, once,
the first time he saw her whole halloween face northeast
across the skating pond as he came down to the ice, December
his seventh year.
     Winter, in this zone,
is an off & on thing, where the air
is sometimes as shining as ice is
when the sky's lights . . .When the ducks
are the only skaters
    And a crèche
is a commerciality

  (The same year, a ball of fire
   the same place—exactly through
   the same trees
   was fire:
     the Sawyer lumber company yard
     was a moon of pain, at the end of itself,
     and the death of horses I saw burning,
     fallen through the floors
     into the buried Blackstone River the city
     had hidden under itself, had grown over

  At any time, & this time
  a city

jangles
  Man's splendor
is a question of which
birth

II

The cries rise, & one of us
has not even eyes to see the night's sky
burning, or the hollows
made coves of mist & frost, the barns
covered over, and nothing in the night but two of us
following the blind highway to catch all glimpses
of the settling, rocking moon

            December, in this year
is a new thing, where I whisper
bye-low, and the pond
is full to its shores again, so full
I read the moon where grass would not reveal it
a month ago, and the ducks make noises
like my daughter does, stir
in the crèche of things

            (His mother, 80, and we
                ate oysters after the burial: we had knelt
                with his sister, now Mary Josephine,
                in the prayery of the convent of the church
                where my mother & father had been married

                And she told us tales of my family
                I had not heard, how my grandfather
                rolled wild in the green grass
                on the banks of that same now underground river
                to cool himself from the steel mill's fires
                stripped down to his red underwear

                she was that gay, to have seen her daughter
                and that the two of us had had that car
                to take the Sisters downtown and drop them
                where they had to go

                            I had watched them
                swirl off in their black habits
                before I started the car again
                in the snow of that street, the same street
                my father had taken me to, to buy my first cap

At any time, & now, again, in this new year
the place of your birth, even a city, rings

in & out of
tune

      What shall be
my daughter's second
birth?

III

All things now rise, and the cries of men to be born
in ways afresh, aside from all old narratives, away
from intervals too wide to mark the grasses

        (not those on which cattle feed, or single stars
        which show the way to buy bad goods
        in green & red lit stores, no symbols

the grasses in the ice, or Orion's sweep, or
the closeness of turning snows, these
can tell the tale of any one of us stormed or quieted
by our own things, what belong, tenaciously,
to our own selves

        Any season, in this fresh time
is off & on to that degree that any of us miss
the vision, lose the instant and decision, the close
which can be nothing more and no thing else
than that which unborn form you are the content of, which you
alone can make to shine, throw that like light
even where the mud was and now there is a surface
ducks, at least, can walk on. And I
have company
in the night

            In this year, in this time
            when spirits do not walk abroad, when men alone walk

            when to walk is so difficult

            when the divine tempter also walks
            renewing his offer—that choice

                    (to turn
            from the gross fire, to hide
            as that boy almost did, to bury himself
            from the fearful face — twice! — that winter

to roll like a dog or his grandfather
in the snowbank on the edge of the pond's ice

to find comfort somewhere, to avoid
the burning — To go to grass
as his daughter now suckles. Some way! he cries out
not to see those horses' agonies:.

       Is light, is there any light, any
       to pay the price of
       fire?

IV

The question stays
in the city out of tune, the skies
not seen, now, again, in
a bare winter time:

       is there any birth
any other splendor than
the brilliance of the going on, the loneliness
whence all our cries arise?

The Leader

They slew him, the women
for the second time he
was meat, the red-headed
man: they served him
to their maws

       (He walked straight into the canyon,
        looked back, looked at them
        and in that glance, by it

They ate him, they did, again, as,
secretly, they seem to have, before
when he was eucharistically present, the boy
was spitted for their wills gone
all teeth

       (He kept ahead, he moved large
        —small in the look of his size
        beneath the sandstone walls—he started up
        the river bed, leaving his back open to

Why they are, and he not loving anything but
his own life, that generousness, that he give
with no expectation of anything back—he,
up to then, often, in the glaring sun had sat
singing out his love, nor found
tranquillity to ease his yearning, always
sleepless cares within his soul wore him
the while he looked for woman's rosy countenance. Instead,
such as these crowded around
and in foul odor and with loud whetted axes
He moved up, out of the shadows
of the lower river, past the white sand,
up ten miles where the water had cut the most
down through the rock, and bottom land,
ten feet off the stream bed, grew peach trees
which glowed from the sun which fell down the sides
of the pinnacle—there, he sang such songs women,
in whose cheeks men's risks raised color,
listened

      while back where he had been his fellows
branded those others that they, disfigured,
would never forget their deed
of hate

To Gerhardt, there, among Europe's things of which he has written us in his "Brief an Creeley und Olson"

so pawed,
by this long last Bear-son

     with no crockery broken,
     but no smile in my mouth

          June 28th, '51, on this horst
          on the Heat Equator, a mediterranean sea
          to the east, and north
          what saves America from desert, waters
          and thus rain-bearing winds,
          by subsidence, salt-waters
             (by which they came,
             the whelps, looking
             for youth

Which they found.
          And have continuously sought

                   to kill

     (o Old Man,

  in winter, when before me, cross my path

  in summer, when behind me, cross my path

  If you want to shut yourself in, shut yourself in
  If you do not want to shut yourself in, come out

          A zoo
          is what he's come to, the old
          Beginner, the old
          Winner

Who took all,
for awhile

(My grandfather, my grandmother,
why have you died?
Did a hand to hand struggle come?
Did a war, the size of a man's fist come?)

1

The proposition, Gerhardt
is to get it straight, right
from the start.

        Help raise the bones
        of the great man.

        Meat and bones we won't throw away.
        We pile it up in a lonely place.

        We do not throw on the ground.
        Your meat and bones without purpose.
        We take bones and meat.

        O Grandfather,
        you went to war

The first duty is
to knock out his teeth, saying
"These are the teeth with which you devour all animals."
I offer you no proper names
either from great cities
on the other side of civilization
which have only to be visited
to be got the hell out of, by bus
or motorcycle, simply because place
as a force is a lie.
or at most a small truth,
now that man has no oar to screw down into the earth, and say
here i'll plant, does not know
why he should cease
staying on the prowl

        You climbed up the tree after some foul berry
        and fell down and died
        You ate berries, fell from the rock
        and died
        You ate sorb berries
        and died
        You ate raspberries,
        drowned in the swamp and died

Or from the other side of time, from a time on the other side of yourself
from which you have so lightly borrowed men, naming them as though,
like your litany of Europe's places, you could take up
their power: magic, my light-fingered faust,
is not so easily sympathetic. Nor are the ladies
worn so decoratively.

> The top of the spring plant
> noisily chewing
>
> The top of the summer plant
> noisily chewing
>
> On a summer day walk before and behind me
> on a winter day

2

Nor can I talk of method, in the face of your letter,
in verse or otherwise,
as though it were a dance
of rains, or schmerz, of words as signs worn
like a toupee on the head of a Poe cast
in plaster, any method otherwise than
he practised it who gave it up,
after a summer in his mother's barn,
because the place smelled so, because time
his time, precisely this now
And with no back references, no
floating over Asia arrogating
how a raiding party moves in advance of a nation, thereby
eventually
giving a language the international power
poets take advantage of. As they also,
with much less reason, from too much economics speak
of the dream
in a peasant's bent shoulders, as though it were true
they cared a damn
for his conversation

> On a mountain with dry stalks, walk
> with a resounding tread
>
> On a mountain with meadow-sweet
> walk with a resounding tread
>
> On the way to your fathers,
> join them

3

Nor of a film, or of strange birds,
or of ordinary ones. Nor with the power of American vocables
would I arm you in Kansas, when you come,
or there, if you have to stay, where you feel so strongly
the dead center of the top of time

                    I am giving you a present

                    I am giving you a present

For you forget (forgetting
is much more your problem
than you know, right-handed one
who so beautifully reminds me
that the birds stand
in the middle of the air
and that always, in that apsed place
in which so many have kneeled
as I do not have the soul to kneel, the fields
are forever harvested, and happy heaven
leans over backwards
to pour its blessings by downfall
on to black earth

Admitting that among the ruins
        with a like schmerz in every vessel of his throat,
        he repeated, "Among the ruins, among them
        the finest memory in the Orient"
one will go about picking up old pieces
        bric-a-brac, he snorted, who did not know whereof he spoke,
        he had so allowed himself to be removed, to back-trail
or put it immediately out of the mind, as some can,
stuff the construction hole quickly with a skyscraper

but you will remember that even Caesar comes to this, certainly you
who has written of Hamlet's death, who is able to handle such large counters
as the classic poet handled bank-notes in our time, before prizes
were his lot, and I am envious, who can do neither
that the point of the rotting of man in his place is also
(beside the long-lived earth of good farmers, its manuring,
what Duncan pointed out America and Russia are very careless with)
what blows about and blocks a hole where the wind was used to go

                    (While walking on the earth with stalks
                    you received a present

While walking on the earth with the stalks of plants
your head was crushed

You could not see, your eyes got small,
you could not defecate, you were small
you could not,
        therefore you died

It is a rod of mountain ash I give you, Rainer Maria Gerhardt,
instead of any other thing, in order that you may also be
left-handed, as he was, your Grandfather,
whom you have all forgotten, have even lost the song of, how
he was to be addressed:

        "Great man,
          in climbing up the tree,
          broke his leg."

I am urging you from here
where nothing is brutal,
not even the old economics
        (I do not dare to breathe
        for what I know the new
        will do) and only the kids kill
frigate-birds, because they have to
to develop a throwing arm

                (as your people knew, if I can lead you
                to go back far enough,
                which is not one step from where you are

                        "His ear is the earth.
                        Let you be careful"

        that he must be hunted, that to eat
        you shall bring him down

                "Your head
                  is the size of a ladle

                Your soul
                  is of the size of a thread

                Do not enter my soul by day,
                do not enter my dreams by night

        that woman—who is, with more resistance
        than you seem to have allowed, named—
        lends herself to him as concubine

what you forget is, you

are their son! You are not

Telemachus. And that you come back

under your own

steam

There are no broken stones, no statues, no images, phrases, composition
otherwise than
what Creeley and I also have,
and without reference to
what reigned in the house
and is now well dismissed

Let you pray to him, we say
who are without such fatherhood:

        "Show your house in spring.

        Show a mound of snow in your house in winter.

        In summer go in back of and in front of
        the children.

        Think not badly of the man, go right."

4

Or come here
where we will welcome you
with nothing but what is, with
no useful allusions, with no birds
but those we stone, nothing to eat
but ourselves, no end and no beginning, I assure you, yet
not at all primitive, living as we do in a space we do not need to contrive

And with the predecessors who, though they are not our nouns, the verbs
are like!

So we are possessed of what you cry over, time
and magic numbers

        Language,
        my enemie,
        is no such system:

> "Hey, old man, the war arrived.
>
> Be still, old man.
>
> Your mouth is shut,
> your door is shut,"

As I said, I am giving you a present.
To all false dimensions,
including his superb one
who refused to allow the social question in,
to all such fathers and false girls
(one of his, I notice, you take, seriously)
why not say what, somewhere, you must hear the echo of?

> "One eye
>   sees heaven,
>   another eye
>   sees earth

For the problem is one of focus, of the field as well as the point of
vision: you will solve your problem best
without displacement

> "One ear
>   hears heaven,
>   another ear
>   hears earth."

In such simplicities I would have you address me,
another time

5

> The old man, my grandfather, died.
> The old woman, my grandmother, died.
> And now my father visits me, clothed
> in a face he never wore, with an odor
> I do not know as his, as his was meadow-sweet.
> He sits, grieving, that she should have worried,
> and I look up at him as he sits there
> and if I am his son, this man
> is from as far a place and time
> as yours is, carries with him
> the strangeness you and I will carry
> for our sons, and for like reason,
> that we are such that can be pawed

"We are no murderers," they used so carefully to say.

"We have put in order the bones of him
whom others kill."

You see, we are experienced of what you speak of: silence
with no covering of ashes, geraniums also
and loaded with aphis

of all but war,

but war, too, is dead as the lotus is dead

And our hardness

has been exaggerated. You see,
we see nothing downward: we walk, as your grandfather walked,
without looking at his feet

"And because of meeting the great man,
a feast is held

Warm yourself,
over the fire of grandfather

This is an offering to the guests, a holiday
of the great man

He will feel satisfied

He will not take revenge

The stick is a reminder, Gerhardt. And the song? what seems
to have been forgotten?

Here it is (as we say here, in our anti-cultural speech, made up
of particulars only, which we don't, somehow, confuse with gossip:

"To his resting place in spring,

to his house in autumn,

I shall go

With autumn plant, arouse the mountain

With spring plant, arouse the mountain

In summer, walk in the background,
do not frighten the children,
do not sniff, neither here
nor there."

A Po–sy, A Po–sy

1

aw, piss, and sing, be
robert burns

Or throw an arm up
in the wind, in the wind's eye,
swing the sail, head
downwards

And look up, hear
the curlew (lost), right straight up
a daisy's ass

    "There is no more time, bro., no more . . .
    t's for tiffins, for the likes of
    yooooooooooou!

    Watch out, CITIZENS, they've
    got you where it hurts
                where it
                     hurts.   "O

    one of those brothers is, o (repeat)
            (go on) "my neigh-bor nooooW (lyrics
    by o—PHEEL—ia: haie high hi!)
                 "one (beat) of (beat)
            THOOOOOSE
    who lived in harlem with everything they ever had (eeeee-
    clectic!)

    And they shat in paper bags.

2

SING! in other words, high! like thistles sound, like "O-
jai, o, O-hi, where the lyyyyr-ick
(low) soooooooules, the (high) faaaaaayk-irs
be, THE
                ooooooooo-RIENT, the ÁWK-ceedent, oH, GOOOOO
west, o. there's NOOOO
rest, there's
only one nest and it's
west

O, there's
NOOOO rest, there's

                        (and repeat and repeat and repeat and reeee-
                        PETE!)

3

yes, my friends, this discussion comes to you as free as
paper bags, comes to you
no permissions granted,
leaves cancelled:x
                Ariadne's silk
s'gone back to
mulberrys

work! bro.: 5 minutes
is all that's necessary to get a fact straight.
Or how will you read a maze
when you see you?

look! sucker: i tellya,
a nose is, a nose is
sure it is, just what you think it is
                WHAT YOU THINK IT IS
                                        wype it,
citizen,
        get on with it

                    The dogs with the fine limbs
are on
                    Here, bro., try to bring an interval down,
at any number of traces
                    See, see, where the blood streams!
And it ain't   in no firmament

    4

no   And my thumb
hurts
      ("What are all these snakes
in her hair?"
                "My god, man, don't you know yr plough
when you hand's on it?")

Try again
to bring her head
round
          (the buoy
is just off yr

plover (lost, also

Who does not fight
will remain unhealed,
no matter how many rains he holds
in his outright palm!

    5

Pansies, it turns out, was a translation

    Dazies, they call 'em, the high-browns

       Medusahatta

(And he didn't know it. But his bigger brother
did. Only, with his bigger brother, it didn't
matta.)

Sd Mrs Henry Adams of Mr Henry James: "Henry
doesn't bite off more than he can chew, he
chews on more than he has bitten off

And then there's the one about time,
wounds all heels

But it's brooks, brooks who makes the proper current
("yr predecessor, my little running water!")

6

In order to be a rock,
start right now ceasing to be
if you are, a twig

Ophelia Flotsam

"And feel yourself to be a
flot-
sum, and feel yrself to be
a
flot   (hold)

sum   (continue)

Settle
right down here, prat in the stream

if you want to be distinguishable,

if you want to be

> "from the ELE-
>   ment, from the
>   ele-
>   MUNT, o

7

balls! Or the image of
3! Sure! it's all over his work. And why not?

What superior direction do you take?
Where's your fin, your stump, former fish?

   item: The vessel walked right off its course and up on the land.

   "O brothers", he cried, "who, after a thousand toils, have
     gained this point of vantage, smell
     the ground!"

8

Soil is of the matter

   Narcissi are

     And the smallest king of an eye
     is a larger thing than a dollar bill!

                 She also sd:

make me a mysterious statue

9

So we have it: Alkinoos,
And three blind lice

(Ya wanta know how? honest-ta-gawd? Well,
rustle that ivory drape

Put your hand on that stucco

Let
yr eye be as light is, when westering, on brick to its east

only
keep a tight hold on
the mast, for

must is a fragrance the earth hath

And we did this incommemorationofhim,
going as the sea went, with only blood
for a thread

END posy END
rime

A Discrete Gloss

The tide, the number 9 and creation
whatever sits outside you is
by what difference what
you also are: this church
or this slaughter house behind it, both
under palms alongside the mud-flats the sea leaves
in front of this three-time city

In what sense is
what happens before the eye
so very different from
what actually goes on within: this man
letting a fat whore hug him in the bus
as it goes counter to the eastering earth,
and I stare, until both of us turn away
as the bus stops and she goes behind it to piss

Your eye, the wanderer, sees more.
Or do you know what it focuses on, what happens
somewhere else: where, say, the sea
is more sea, and men
do not take Saturday Sunday off, arguing
they need to clean the gurry, a boat
takes that much drying, that much
sun

When the field of focus
is not as admitted as the point is,
what loss!   Who loves
without an object, who dreams
without an incubus, who fears
without cause?   Or dies
without all animalness, the disgorging
of breath blood bowels so tenderly
who can say the affections
are not the conquerors?

That what we do with what we are
is what ends all distraction.
As fiercely as the eye
is fierce.   Or death
is fierce.   Who cares
that they have taught us otherwise,
that they still noise it about
there are abstract things, human birds
with wings which only once
(in Giotto's hands) made
black and orange sense?

You who can seize
as the sun seizes.   Who drinks
by a stem as brilliant as that stopless eater of flowers. Who acts
as swiftly as a plant turns light to green. Or this chameleon's throat
wops red red red and why
I do not know, but that he does, that you do
that you can take some human thigh bone you've picked up
and with a stone tool carve such likeness on it
as much conjecture as the man you draw
was Quetzalcoatl more a sea-horse than himself—
such as you makes gorging nature at her blackest root
a silly starer too.

The day of man returns in your precisions, kin
(ahau, katun), the force
of force where force forever is
and man forgets: what is the world
that he can separate himself so simply from it,
or their soul, that I can locate it, or your act
that you can say its cause?

Man is no creature of his own discourse:
here on this beach made by the tide which passed
and dragged away old guts (or the birds
had it before the fish fed) and he turned, I turned
away, where nine madereros left a politician cut and stoned for dead
(where she pissed), it can be seen
that these boats dry in colours only he
had an eye for. And it says, it says here
in the face of everything it says
this, is the more exact

Concerning Exaggeration, or
How, Properly, to Heap Up

1

About blood, he said, be
more circumspect, for that matter,
these days, about anything
has been cried in the streets. We are called on
to correct all
economies

I am not my parts. I am one system,
affect all others, act, and express myself as such, wild
or indifferent

2

Or birth. ("He with the squint cried aloud.") She
came up out of a wave caused by the fall of her father's parts
neatly sickled off by a brother as handsome as she. Another
was hid in his father's thigh, was hid from a jealous wife,
before his natural mother bore him. A third
was an egg, was born of an egg because his mother was too old,
and built a city in a night, protected only
by a cap of bread

No wonders: the sun
crawls down the tree's branches and through the roots into the earth
each might, and there are tigers there
which can eat it

                a man
who had mastered all languages but Arabic
broke a friend's skull with a shovel just
for some silver plate, though he excused himself
saying, the friend had been familiar
with his wife

              Or he
who was as fleet as the herds he'd run his life with,
had to be taught by a courtesan human speech
in order that he might enter the city
and put an end to the Leader's lusts

                                                or that one
who came back from the war to find his double
was in the house and bed and even had a mole
in the right place, the man was so confused
he wondered who he was

3

The head, too. I look around me, and I find two, only two
who are as he was who wore a hawk on the back of his neck, the wings
curved round the sides of the head to frame the brilliant
human face, the muteness arguing, the muteness of both,
that this one at least, this leader,
was informed, was recognizing other force
than that which one might call
his own

        As it was for me in a dream
        when I was a horse on both sides of a river
        and a lady of flowers, and another, laid hands on me,
        each on each side

                Or that night my friend the dramatist
        arranged us all in a charade so that two of us
        passed through the door a centaur while a huge murderess
        fed water-lilies gently to crocodiles

                        And I twist,
                        in the early morning, asking
                        where
                        does it stop

4

All, is of the matter. Dignity
is not to be confused with realism, is not found
(he was canny enough to say)
in the straight-on

                however much it does lie
in particulars—as distorted as an instant is, is
content. And its form? How shall you find it
if you are not, in like degree, allowable, are not
as it is, at least, in preparation for
an equal act?

And, if this is true,
how can you avoid the conclusion, how
can you be otherwise than
a metaphor
            than as fabulous as to move
except as your own fingers duplicate
a long-nailed god, your eye
to be so trained by night
it goes as slow as weights
(as slow as Shiva's turning toe), as fast—how run
except as he did (as tern flies), how gauge yourself
except as also Cenozoic beast (as she is afterwards,
no more than tired animal, who speaks
as how else can you too speak
except as she listened who hunched
over those craters and caked pools drunk
from the earth's gases, and said
he has put tortoises
under twelve gold covers
on twelve gold plates

        To speak of blood
        is so very willful,
        or self-incising. In any case,
        he who is presented with her answer is
        that answer: the mephitic
        is only confirmatory. Yet
        the vapor of those instants
        —blood, breath, head, what—
        require like
        circumspection

                (was what he said,
                 at that point of
                 his time)

Merce of Egypt

1   I sing the tree is a heron
    I praise long grass.
    I wear the lion skin
    over the long skirt
    to the ankle. The ankle
    is a heron

    I look straightly backward. Or I bend to the side straightly
    to raise the sheaf
    up the stick of the leg
    as the bittern's leg, raised
    as slow as
    his neck grows
    as the wheat. The presentation,
    the representation,
    is flát,

    I am followed by women and a small boy in white carrying a duck,
    all have flat feet and, foot before foot, the women with black wigs
    And I intent
    upon idlers,
    and flowers

2   the sedge
    as tall as I am, the rushes
    as I am

        as far as I am animal, antelope
    with such's attendant carnivores

                      and rows of beaters
    drive the game to the hunter, or into nets,
    where it is thick-wooded or there are open spaces
    with low shrubs

3 I speak downfall, the ball of my foot
   on the neck of the earth, the hardsong
   of the rise of all trees, the jay
   who uses the air. I am the recovered sickle
   with the grass-stains still on the flint of its teeth.
   I am the six-rowed barley
   they cut down.

   I am tree. The boy of the back of my legs
   is roots. I am water fowl
   when motion is the season of my river, and the wild boar
   casts me. But my time
   is hawkweed,

4 I hold what the wind blows, and silt.
   I hide in the swamps of the valley to escape civil war,
   and marauding soldiers. In the new procession
   I am first, and carry wine
   made of dandelions. The new rites
   are my bones

   I built my first settlement
   in groves

5   as they would flail crops
   when the spring comes, and flood, the tassels
   rise, as my head

Knowing All Ways,
Including the Transposition
of Continents

I have seen enough: ugliness
in the streets,
and in the flesh I love

I have gone as far as I will go: justice
is not distributable, outside
or in

I have had all I intend
of cause or man: the unselected
(my own) is enough
to be bothered with. Today
I serve beauty of selection alone
—and without enormous reference to stones
or to the tramp of worms
in the veins. Image
can be exact to fact, or
how is this art twin to what is,
what was,
what goes on?

America, Europe, Asia,
I have no further use for you: your clamor
divides me from love,
and from new noises.

The Morning News

> "O mister Eckhart! calling
> Meister Eck-heart!
>
> "Doctor Strzygowski!"
>
> ". . . truly hermetique,
> Nothing catholique . . ."
>
> Natura NON morte:
> it was a bowl of fruit
> (I am no hero and no saint,
> nor are we scamps
> or crockery-breakers)
> a bowl, a golden bowl, in any day,
> put out there, on the table, as jewels
> were worn, in fact, as the fine birds
> were wrought, the pair of peacocks' heads,
> say, set with the Syrian garnets

Neither to be eaten nor

to be made pretty of.

1

"One of the less known names of that Omaha chief known to history as Handsome Slayer was, He-Who-Runs-Away-To-Play-Another-Day. He was one of the founders of that curious Indian society which called itself the Backward Boys. It was a special Plains society, of which the members did everything, including the carrying of a lance and the riding of their horses, backwards.

"It was rumored that, and it is now thought that, there were hidden sexual motivations for this strange behavior. It is true, that all Indian life, particularly that of the Plains Indians of North America, exhibits a violence which the modern mind, now that it has been given the proper tools, cannot avoid seeing as repressive in origin. It is only now becoming clear, for example, that the war-whoop, which seemed to the early settlers to be only a device of what we would now call 'psychological warfare', was, in truth, nothing but an obvious sign of Indian arrestment at a pre-Oedipean level.

"We are just beginning now to do adequate research into this interesting orality."

I remember the day. It was not too many years ago. Spring was on me so (it was a Sunday afternoon, April, perhaps) that I persisted, when my friends insisted, that I come inside and be present while they entertained their girls at cocktails, I persisted in the sun and sat long alone on the grass.

But here is the point. When I did come in I was so caught up in the afflatus of that season

        Aprille with her arrowes sweete
that I sat plump down between the two ladies, and took them both in my arms.

At which point, and since that day (one of the ladies later became the wife of one of my friends) those two buddies of mine have been consistently and hiddenly, my enemies!

          And who shall say
I was not possibly, like that old Indian chief,
p.sy-kick?   who'll
deny to this brief vigil of our senses, knowledge
of what's inside us?

            (Will you,
            old Armourer?

            or you,
            my Captain of the Hold?

            for look! look! where the blood
              has ceased to run
            in the collapsed veins!

2

"Though it is Easter, this is, alas,—we must face it, be brave,
remember *all* our Lessons—the day of *no* light. This is, in
short, the Gray Day.   All we can do is, quietly, each for
himself, weep."

    Listen, bro. What you better remember is,

    when she passes, you tip your hat!

    We are such trembling vapours

    as trains are run on. Do not count

    the telegraph poles.

    And if you can bounce high,

    do that too, until she cry,

    "Lover, gold-hatted, high-bouncing lover,

    you come over here!"

                    (Hold! o Amor-eur!

                    I, too, wear
                    the Visored Face.)

3

"What desolation! I cannot stand

yr new

civilization!"   (What a shot
                    that was!)

    You who have stayed too long at the oar-locks,

    look now—or you'll never see its like again!

    The rails are layed down, and even the engine's

    got its steam up. Don't, Pearl,

    lay yrself across the tracks!

        (And he sped, red-hot, over the seas,

          put a belt around the earth,

          and all this before the Supreme Court could say,

        Dred Scott!)

4

The sun sat there,
like a great squash.

And by god if the two of 'em,
with their spread fat arses,
didn't try to squush
me!

Who the the hell are they to say

        "Th-is,

            is go-ing to beeeeee

       a GRRRR-eat

         DAY!"

     And we used to do it,
     at dawn on the deck,
     and toss the bucket overboard,
     dowsing it a couple of times
     to be sure it was clean

     What I remember most
     is the smell of Shea's tobacco.
     And his talking, before breakfast,
     of "Kunrudd", as he pronounced it,
     of Kunrudd, and that book
     whose title he could never get straight.

(Come to think of it, it was Red Flaming who sd,

desolation. I'm not so sure he doesn't show

some of the old blood. For he is, with all his strength,

one of the Boys.

     There was this conversation:
     "Can you tell a dawn when you see one?"
     "Aw, a pock a lips! Gimme no more of yr jaw!"
     It remined me of what the old man used to say:
     "Put a tackle on it, it's
     hangin',
     son!"

I gathered what he meant was, the chin. When the chin is large (this is already clear to Fenichel and other excellent doctors like him) it is a sign that there has been too much eating going on, even though it can come just as much from self-satisfaction as from actual cannibalism.

"This is now so apparent that there is no longer any need to study further the institution, among the tribes, of what can best be translated as Saint Stephen's Rite. Stephen is interesting as the founder, as the first one with genius enough to see how necessary it was in a hunting society that a masticatory image be provided to the people so that they might understand what they were doing with their daily lives.

"Like so much of the late Metastatic culture . . .".

WE BREAK OFF
THE INTELLECTUAL PART OF THIS PROGRAM TO
BRING YOU A SPECIAL AND MOMENTOUS NEWS
BULLETIN!

"Cibola has fallen!

The Anthropophagi are

IN COMPLETE RETREAT!!!!"

AND NOW the poet HAS AN IMPORTANT MESSAGE
FOR YOU!

THE POET: "O! seven cities!
That made this country great!
Whose skies, *profumo,* blotted out the sun!

"O! seven cities!

Who once so poisoned all our children that

they opened out, *colombo,* all the West!

"O seven cities! Now

that you lie down together,

fortissimo, deny not,

(o God, Smog of our Fathers)

your glorious wrongs!"

THANK YOU, LAUREATE!

IN ADDITION, AT THIS WAKE-UP HOUR,

WE BRING YOU—

　　　　THE HANDSOME SAILOR!

　　　　　　　(*Crowd noises*:　　"sesquipedentifrice
　　　　　　sesquipedentifrice　　sesquipedentifrice"

　　　　　　and *shouts* of:　　"Fer cryssake, he
　　　　　　　　　　　　　　won't TALK!

　　　　　　　　　　　　　　"Look! the dope, he
　　　　　　　　　　　　　　STUTTERS!"

　　　　　　and *all*: "KILL 'im, KILL 'IM"

　　　　no, citizens,

　　　　no

　　　　　　　(*musical bridge,* in, & over:

　　　　"This is
　　　　　　　th-is is,
　　　　　　　　　　the NEWooo
　　　　Da-YYYYY!"

6

　　　　And they cuffed him

　　　　And our tears were as gold

　　　　"It is cold here
　　　　You must go out and bring in some wood
　　　　For there is much to be done."

　　　　And we obeyed her,
　　　　because she was old,
　　　　and our mother.

　　　　　　　END
　　　　　　　broadcast

I, Mencius, Pupil of the Master . . .

the dross of verse. Rhyme!
when iron (steel)
has expelled Confucius
from China. Pittsburgh!
beware: the Master
bewrays his vertu
To clank like you do
he brings coolie verse
to teach you equity,
who layed down such rails!

Who doesn't know a whorehouse
from a palace (who doesn't know the Bowery
is still the Bowery, even if it is winos
who look like a cold wind, put out their hands
to keep up their pants

        that the willow or the peach blossom
        ...Whistler, be with America
        at this hour

        open galleries. And sell
        Chinese prints, at the opening,
        even let the old ladies in—

        let decoration thrive, when
        clank is let back
        into your song

           when voluntarism
        abandons
        poetic means

Noise! that Confucius himself
should try to alter it, he
who taught us all
that no line must sleep,
that as the line goes so goes
the Nation! that the Master
should now be embraced by the demon
he drove off!   O Ruler

in the time of chow,
that the Soldier
should lose the Battle!

that what the eye sees,
that in the East the sun untangles itself
from among branches,
should be made to sound as though there were still roads
on which men hustled
to get to paradise, to get to
Bremerton
shipyards!

II

that the great 'ear
can no longer 'hear!

o Whitman,
let us keep our trade with you when
the Distributor
who couldn't go beyond wood,
apparently,
has gone out of business

let us not wear shoddy
mashed out of
even the Master's
old clothes, let us bite off Father's
where the wool's
got too long (o Solomon Levi

in your store on Salem Street,
we'll go there to buy our ulsterettes,
and everything else that's neat

III

We'll to these woods
no more, where we were used
to get so much, (Old Bones
do not try to dance

go still
now that your legs

the Charleston
is still for us

                              You can watch
It is too late
to try to teach us

                  we are the process
                          and our feet

                                  We do not march
We still look
            And see
                  what we see

                          We do not see
                          ballads
other than our own.

Anecdotes of the Late War

1. the lethargic vs violence as alternatives of each other for los americanos

> & US Grant (at Shiloh, as ex.) had the gall to stay
> inside a lethargy until it let him down into either
> vice (Galena, or, as president) or
> a virtue of such a movement as, example,
> Vicksburg

> say that he struck, going down, either
> morass or
> rock—and when it was rock, he was

—this wld seem to be the power in the principle—

able to comprehend to movement of mass of men, the

transposition of the

Mississippi (Or

continents, example,

somebody else than:

grant

> better, that is, that a man stay lethargic than

blow somebody's face off—off,

the face of, blow

the earth

2. that (like the man sd) Booth
   killing Lincoln is the melodrama right with
   the drama: Mister Christ and
   Broadway

> Or going out to Bull Run looking for
> Waterloo. the
> diorama. And having to get the fastidious hell home

that afternoon
as fast as the carriage horses
can't make it (Lee Highway
littered with broken
elegances

         Reverse of
sic transit gloria, the
Latin American whom the cab driver told me
he picked up at Union Station had
one word of english—link-
cone. And drove him
straight to the monument, the man
went up the stairs and fell down on his knees
where he could see the statue and stayed there
in the attitude of prayer

3. whoop,
   went the bird
   in the tree the day
   the fellow
   fell down
   in the thicket

   whoop, was the bird's
   lay as the fellow lay

   and I picked up a minie ball
   (the way
   it can be
   again
   of an afternoon,

   or with the French girl Brandy Station
   was
   thick grass
   and the gray house and back of it

   yes   man   the   movement

   of horses, as

   —I repeat—

   the bird.

4. West Point is wasn't. Nor New England. Nor
   those cavalry
   flauntlets

      As the Mexican War was
   filibusterers
   in the West,
   and cadets
   before Chapultepec: the elevator

      goink down

      from waterloo,

      the Civil War

was the basement. Only nobody

except butternut

and his fellow on the other side

wanted to believe it, they all wanted

what Jay Gould got

(and Joe Blow got swap
in the side of the head

5. Now you take this Forrest, Nathan Bedford Forrest. He stalks the Western
   theater of operations as something the English, to this day, think Lee
   wouldn't have surpassed had anybody dared to give this Memphis slave-
   trader the width of men and field to command which he only had as
   first Grand Wizard of the Ku Klux Klan. And didn't use, Forrest
   could already avoid the temptation of the Filibuster, he had applied
   first principles in the War.

   What I'd wanted to say was,
   that he's a man so locked in the act of himself

      (right up to after Davis had been taken
   and no last movie scene to the way he was still
   cutting tracks behind U. S. Army units, a very

   exact and busy man.

I also have to voice this impression of him to give, if it
does, the sense of how he was:

> he's like a man his tongue was cut out,
> before even Shiloh showed him
> an extraordinary executive
> of men horses and goods

6. Two things still aren't brought in to give context to the War: (1), that
   you don't get Grant except as you find what he was that Geo Washington
   also comes alive at only if you realize he was to real estate—

                              and I mean land
when land was as oil steel and what, now?

Managing men, wasn't it, when men suddenly what was Grant's

because of the industrial revolution

were what the guys who died then were

                              For the first time,
like that, the sprawled fellow Devil's Glen, natural
resource.

        The other half of it—(2)—that each one of them,

Butternut,

and Yankee Doodle,

weren't as different as North and South, farmer and factory etc.

They were—for the first time—enough of them.

                              Plus railroad tracks
                              to be moved around as
utility
        The leaders,   Grant Sherman Forrest not
                                     Jeb Stuart
        and themselves

        the birth of

                    the recent   And Lincoln

                    likewise   (after Christ

                    Link-cone

7. You take it
    from there

8. What he said was, in that instance
    I got there first
    with the most men

    Grant didn't hurry.
    He just had the most.

    More of the latter died.

The Death of Europe

(a funeral poem for Rainer M. Gerhardt)

Rainer,
the man who was about to celebrate his 52nd birthday
the day I learned of your death at 28, said:
"I lie out on Dionysius' tongue"!

the sort of language you talked, and I did,
correctingly—
           as I heard this other German wrongly,
from his accent, and because I was thinking of you,
talking of how much you gave us all hearing
in Germany (as I watch a salamander on the end of a dead pine branch
snagging flies), what I heard this man almost twice your age say was,
"I lie out on a dinosaur's tongue"!

for my sense, still, is that,
despite your sophistication
and your immense labors . . .

It will take some telling. It has to do with what WCW
(of all that you published in *fragmente*, to see Bill's
R R BUMS in futura!

                    it has to do with how far back are

Americans,
as well as,
Germans

                "walk on spongy feet
                if you would cross

                carry purslane
                if you get into her bed

                guard the changes
                when you scratch your ear

I

It is this business
that you should die!
Who shot up,
out of the ruins,
and hung there,
in the sky,
the first of Europe
I could have words with:

as Holderlin on Patmos you
trying to hold bay leaves
on a cinder block!

                    Now I can only console you,
                    sing of willows,
                    and dead branches,
                    worry the meanness
                    that you do not live,
                    wear the ashes
                    of loss

                         Neither of us
                    carrying a stick
                    any more

Creeley told me
how you lived

II

I have urged anyone
back (as Williams asked
that Sam Houston
be recognized
                    as I said,
Rainer, plant
your ash

     "I drive a stake into the ground, isn't it silly,"
I said out loud in the night, "to drive a stake into the ground?"

How primitive
does one have to get? Or,

as you and I were both open
to the charge: how large

can a quote

get, he

said, eyeing me

with a blue

eye

        Were your eyes

        brown, Rainer?

        Rainer,

        who is in the ground,

        what did you look like?

        Did you die of your head bursting

        like a land-mine?

        Did you walk

        on your own unplanted self?

III

It is not hell you came into,
or came out of. It is not moly
any of us are given. It is merely
that we are possessed of
the irascible. We are blind
not from the darkness
but by creation we are
moles. We are let out
sightless, and thus miss
what we are given, what woman
is, what your two sons
looking out of a picture at me,
sitting on some small hillside—

they have brown eyes, surely.

Rainer, the thyrsus
is down

I can no longer
put anything
into your hands

It does no good
for me to wish
to arm you

I can only carry laurel,
and some red flowers,
mere memorials, not cut
with my own knife an oar
for you, last poet
of a civilization

You are nowhere
but in the ground

IV

What breaks my heart
is that your grandfather
did not do better, that our grandmothers
(I think we agreed)
did not tell us
the proper tales

so that we are as raw
as our inventions, have not the teeth
to bite off Grandfather's
paws

(O, Rainer,
you should have ridden your bike
across the Atlantic instead of your mind,
that bothered itself too much
with how we were hanging on
to the horse's tail, fared, fared

we who had Sam Houston, not
Ulysses

I can only cry: Those
who gave you not enough

caused you to settle for
too little

         The ground
is now the sky

     v

But even Bill
is not protected,
no swift messenger
puts pussley
even in his hand,
open,

as it is, no one says how
to eat
at the hairy table

       (as your scalp
also lifted,
      as your ears
did not stay

silk

         O my collapsed brother,
the body
does bring us
down
      The images
have to be
contradicted
         The metamorphoses
are to be
undone

The stick,
and the ear

are to be no more than

they are: the cedar

and the lebanon

of this impossible

life.

I give you no visit

to your mother.

What you have left us

is what you did

It is enough

It is what we

praise

I take back

the stick.

I open my hand

to throw dirt

into your grave

I praise you

who watched the riding

on the horse's back

It was your glory to know

that we must mount

O that the Earth

had to be given to you

this way!

O Rainer, rest

in the false

peace

Let us who live

try

Proensa

FOR Creeley and Blackburn

here, a Sunday, when light
is fall's
whiteness
        when no smallness
(of even a bed) contains
the affairs of men (when not even Salonika
one can be count of, or marry
Constantine's niece, in Cyprus, and sport
imperial arms)

and yet one does know
an air to suck, and where,
in six inches, shafts
of the sun have fallen
in such manner they
stay as the straight body they
sang, because we,
by usage and by nature, also
have known
        what they were as clear in as
(Peking,
had less important
things

If love was
(when fighting was, when the heart
was eaten
to correct
national abuses,

if love was
so clearly sung, and sirventes
did serve
to stir things up

And now they don't

Ladies
are not to be abandoned,
are forever
abandoned,
                    the clothes
we wrap love in,
we are to be hunted, until
we, too, are brought to our mistresses's
bed, to be laughed over
for the clothes we wear

    And to be cured
    (by her and her husband)
    as our tongue
    was also once cut,

    and healed enough meanwhile,
    for us to sing with

The Cause, the Cause

It is the cause the cause, still, it is (and she, still
even though the method be
new, be
the rods and cones of, a pigeon's or, a rabbit's
eye, or be
who, man, is that woman you now dream of, who
woman, is that
man

named & featured, yet
who it is you sit beside, each of you, there, by the bubbling caldron in which bones
and furniture are tossed (a grisly soup from which child's fingers drop, flames
spill out
on treacherous ground across which he leads you, i
lead you on, in,
a devils', angels'
dancings, the measured feet (clean, & sweet as hair is, used
to dry an ankle, toes
                    hair, wild quiet hair crushed
where cylinder & amulet compose
no dream
increasing rhein timed to come closer, closer
repeat, repeat, as regular as

                    by that fire you sit you dream, you two, you
talk about some other

2

it is the cause, yes, and the movements contain, the nightmare is
the day's ambiguous responses, her
harassments, his
flying off, his sort of looking out by cones, is it, or is it old, like bones
anyway, his
watchings
where the arc is now being pushed, can be, pushed, her
unreasonable opinions, her
subjects so badly introduced, her rods, her
in the eye, in the eye of his will, her
multiple witholdings, her
not at all dumb dance, her measurings

3

put it this way (to make the case specific, as well as, historic: he
smothered her
because he could not free his half self from her likeness, carried (jealous)
buried, you can say, and no more mirroring her — no, not at all, in fact
a she, initiate with himself alone. another creature concealed in him —
a female male to him his confusion — made male by one point short majority

and thus
          (no confirmation offered, proferred him by his grown unround world

                ((his world become a rotted apple, no light
                  on why, at this queer juncture, he should find himself a
                  double

halved, in his own eye, halved, he
cried out for love of her, pressed down, pressed down, and —
crown of his no longer endurable, not sufficiently regular
pain, he
killed this other
for half love of another
Eve

4

nor is this all. nor is the story (upper case) so small
as he, and she, alone. in fact it is, there is, another half, the tragedy
repeats itself in inverse, increasing inverse (transvest) plane:

                  on this even more rotted stage, the rage —
no longer only male (the half's gone over!) repeats, repeats!

for woman, too, is joined & sundered, returned
is now (alas) — she, too — returned
to mono-beast, she too conceals a brother

And from the Cain once seen, in the light suddenly on the edge of the pot, jumping
from the fire up, recognized—
again,
murder, another
murder

5

To murder to be free from incubus when difference, difference only
is the cause (the cause here spoiled)

All form and essence both brought down, mixed, in this middle place, this
where there is neither one nor the other, this by man and woman dirtied, this
fouled place

But still the cause, it is the cause by which things stand
(by which all eyes are two, and in fact the day by night
stand, all moving things are made to stay, to stay in place, are bought
together

what they are, what a dream is, a man a woman are
the hidden others of which they themselves are the face, by

a hair of difference, are
no greater difference than,
the cause, is
life from its own ending

Love

(down,
to my soul:

                assume your nature as yourself,
                for the love of God

                          not even good enough

Stories
        only
            the possibility
                 of discrete
                      men

There is no intelligence
the equal of
the situation

There are only
            two ways:
            create the situation
                    (and this is love)
            or avoid it.
                This also can be

Love.

The Motion

the motion
not verbal
      the newt
      less active
             than I: the fire pink
             not me
                    (the words
                    not me

not my nature
I
      Not even honor
      anything
             but that my freshness
             not be opened
                (as my mail must not be, before I do.

No doctrine
      even that the flower flames
                  if I don't. No capture
if the captive,
      even the instant,
             is not I.

Thus thou.

The Pavement

the pavement
I take so long
to go along by

      the walk
      from the house
      to the store

            I can't jump over

The obduracy
of spirit, the doubt
of person, the locus
only the place
I was not conceived in

      Only where I was named
      because I was known
      for the first time

            to be there. And I
            unknown

And
who am I

      any more than

            who knows

the lines

      I break my father's spine,

            the cracks

I break my mother's back

      are so wide,

            they are not so easily

Used.

Asymptotes

yup, our disgraces are
our Graces

nor have i a talent,
or a virtue,
to lend

i, too, am retted down, am
mere aroid,
like a cuckoopint decide
i am all spike and bract

for who has time
to undo his ignorance?
have you?
may i stop you,
may i tap you on the shoulder

                        say, have you got a match,
                        Prometheus?

                        what was it like,
                        to be bound?

                        in your winter, what fed
                        on your liver, Ambiguous?

myself, i go by glee,
don't even know the bird
eats me

(o for a beak,
                    (Hail, Claw!

to be sharp!

The Post Virginal

$F = ci^2$ Keats: the intensity of object   The trouble
with symbol,

it does not trouble. One is the product of one TIMES
one. And that a new object . . . that the blue eyes
can't see their own face

don't mean they don't look. In fact
the law of times is, that a discrimination
is only restored by the multiplication
of each discrimination by another, no matter
how many it takes. Even if it is one,
it is multiplied by itself. This is known
as discontent.

                                   That all things recur
is not the equal of the fact that they occur (God
is interesting in three ways:

            that he invented so much, that he invented so little
            and that so much of so little occurs anew

Waste, limit & mortality

These are the powers.
                      There are two classes.
There are those who have by having what there is to have.
These are they who suffer. Suffering is a medium
which doesn't have the relief
of talent. Desire without form begets

Form is not life. Form is creation. It changes the condition
of men. It does not disturb nature. Nature, like god,
is not so interesting. Man

is interesting

For a man gone to Stuttgart
who left an automobile behind him

a Lost Poem by Charles Olson, for JW, to inaugurate the book

                  the callacanthus
out again (the golden fury seen
thru those red candles

not at all a dead car, curiously,
even though it hasn't moved as what pushes out buds
has

not deadhead (as Grady's
two were, all winter

Beyond, the grove of little dogwood (today's
entry

      But, by the heady red flowers (their smell
will be heavy), the large dogwood (the single bush,
back of the stone steps,
glares

and it came out this way (just after you had left,
a year ago

suddenly the spring field is blue, of figwort
and the callacanthus smell is intercepted by that color
as the dogwood was by the green of my pleasure
that I slept under it, for an hour, and woke,
as they have, to the rising of
the forces

Variations done for
Gerald Van De Wiele

I. LE BONHEUR

dogwood flakes
what is green

the petals
from the apple
blow on the road

mourning doves
mark the sway
of the afternoon, bees
dig the plum blossoms

the morning
stands up straight, the night
is blue from the full of the April moon

iris and lilac, birds
birds, yellow flowers
white flowers, the Diesel
does not let up dragging
the plow

        as the whippoorwill,
the night's tractor, grinds
his song

        and no other birds but us
are as busy (O saisons, o chateaux!

Délires!

        What soul
is without fault?

Nobody studies
happiness

Every time the cock crows
I salute him

I have no longer any excuse
for envy. My life

has been given its orders: the seasons
seize

the soul and the body, and make mock
of any dispersed effort. The hour of death

is the only trespass

II. THE CHARGE

dogwood flakes
the green

the petals from the apple-trees
fall for the feet to walk on

the birds are so many they are
loud, in the afternoon

they distract, as so many bees do
suddenly all over the place

With spring one knows today to see
that in the morning each thing

is separate but by noon
they have melted into each other

and by night only crazy things
like the full moon and the whippoorwill

and us, are busy. We are busy
if we can get by that whiskered bird,

that nightjar, and get across, the moon
is our conversation, she will say

what soul
isn't in default?

can you afford not to make
the magical study

which happiness is? do you hear
the cock when he crows? do you know the charge,

that you shall have no envy, that your life
has its orders, that the seasons

seize you too, that no body and soul are one
if they are not wrought

in this retort? that otherwise efforts
are efforts? And that the hour of your flight

will be the hour of your death?

III. SPRING

The dogwood
lights up the day

The April moon
flakes the night.

Birds, suddenly,
are a multitude

The flowers are ravined
by bees, the fruit blossoms

are thrown to the ground, the wind
the rain forces everything. Noise—

even the night is drummed
by whippoorwills, and we get

as busy, we plow, we move,
we break out, we love. The secret

which got lost neither hides
nor reveals itself, it shows forth

tokens. And we rush
to catch up. The body

whips the soul. In its great desire
it demands the elixir

In the roar of spring,
transmutations. Envy

drags herself off. The fault of the body and the soul
—that they are not one—

the matutinal cock clangs
and singleness: we salute you

season of no bungling

Queen Street Burle-Q

Rose LaRose

    in the purple light on stage

working up a milk-shake

       turbulent
       frothy

without any need of

    milk and/or shaker

I believe in you . . .

     you & Rimbaud,
you are right to love the Great Mother

And to despair in a time when Kore only
(when Demeter has to be looked for

when only the Maiden (when woman
does not know she is also who hunts
for herself
    Instead of finding half herself
in every ad.

There is no hell when hell is
toothpaste. And Demeter

Oh, Woman:
lay about you!
    Slay!
      That you may have cause again
to seek yourself, to go out among flowers crying
"Kore! Kore!", knowing

the King of Hell
also has you

The Loves of Anat, 1

Anat and Acbat
Said Anat
loan me your

Said Acbat
you sneaky female

At which Anat
was wrought

and went to the Lord God
That Acbat

won't let me borrow his
he called me a virgin

El, will you give him
hell?

Christmas

dirty Christmas
which Origen
and Clement
both showed up

for the junk it
is—as though,
sd O, he was a
mere Pharoah. Or,

says Clement, do
we have here some
child baptism to
go gew-gaw over?

in long favorably
embroidered gown,
a boy? instead of
a man standing

in desire in the
Jordan, with green
banks on either
side, a naked man

treated by another
adult man who also
has found that
to be as harmless

as a dove is what
a man gets as wise
as a serpent for,
the river,

of life?

O'Ryan 1

Overall, mover of the unnumbered

_____

who did twelve labors, rose
at 4 A M. And when I complained
that I could not do as much,
she turned it on me this way,
that if he went to bed at 2
and rose at 4, you
rise at 2
and go to bed at 4. I thinking,
how neat. And necessary, we
who don't have God to encourage us,
at least that aim
in the business. Or think women
as much as those did who had God
We love em, we do not do without em
our necks are bent, we do see
the reflection, we do know
who's who, how what we ride
rides us, how there are twelve houses
to be got through: what one are you at,
fellow fellow?   My purpose

is to invoke you, not at all any
muse.   Or at least none
that you are beholden
to, that you know
by taking sight, by merely
looking up. No zodiac
neither the one which comes after
pleasure, nor that one
after labors. The cincture now,
the emblem of the championship,
is care—by your mother's fire.
And sleep—sometime sodden sleep.

I don't read your face. Or you mine.
By looking up or down. Neither
the light nor the dark do we brawn
by. We do it all, I take it, my
fellow.
                    Will you join me
in one on the house?

                    Shall we drink
to the ladies?

O'Ryan 2

Tell me something, tell me
how you got that way

how'dya lose your
what stuck you in the pants

why did they ask you
to take on so much

Tell me something, tell me
what made you do it

why did you buy
so much shit

how come you got so far off
the rail

tell me, where are you
nowadays, what makes you

look so warm in the eye, who
told you your flesh is

as rosy as your
baby's, as rosy as

Rosy, as, your
moth-er's, as who got you up

in the morning
in the morning

Tell me: how'dya
get up?   how did you

stand up after all
that lying down

what took
that look off

your face, how come you
shine, no shine

at all, all white
and looking all over

hey, bruiser: tell me

something

O'Ryan 3

I heard they got you
on a rape charge

Or was it mugging
Or just minding

your own business, that you looked too much
like your fellow men?

was it they burned you
on the yellow tree?

O'Ryan 4

The story starts. It's
cinema
      Mah
Or chuck, chuck, I'll
play with your rosy

Kate's the girl for a
sail-
        or for a

bosun, a gunner, a-
merican (heave me a

sigh, he said, I lost
her, I lost her

by saying too much
by opening my mouth

And who comes along
but a sly guy, a guy

who doesn't do anything but
sigh—and of course

she was his, of course

We couldn't love you
if we didn't love you

with our mouth shut

O'Ryan 5

In other words
there ain't no villain
in this piece,
none at all.

There isn't any,
anyway.   You find me one.

who isn't some stinking
sonofabitch of a man

O'Ryan 6

Your mother's. Your
mother's like they say

in a Chinese novel, to be as straight about it
as a sign can

As a sign in a can

We begin,
that way.

Virgin.
            OK.

And let her rest, let her
if you can give it to her

if you can give it to her soul, if you can find out
what you owe her, what peace

a woman is, how you are all there
or you ain't, you haven't

slaked her thirst, you haven't
What a man has to do, he has to

meet his mother in hell

O'Ryan 7

Woman is a man's
all cause

A man don't have
no other

He can look, he's got
plenty, it's a short

he's got all the sky
to get up into, to get off his

But a woman is a man's
   yes
      yes
         yes

O'Ryan 8

He was all lit up
like a pinball machine

a son of the working
classes

He came down on her
in the middle of the road

he belted her, he pinned his shoulders
to her

And he scowled
right through his back

O'Ryan 9

It's that way that's all
whether you like it or not

even if you can get it
all prettied up

Or you're that damned fool literate
you buy store bought clothes

Don't fool yourself
Underneath all them poems

it's night

you got a hard on

and it's

to be made

He loved a girl
And her name was Woods.

He wooed her in the Maytime,
he wooed her in the fall

He wooed her after all the others,
he wooed her in his shoes,
he wooed her in the creases
between his rotten toes

He wooed her even though
she threw the book at him
he ran as fast as he could run
to keep his first look at her bum

She knew her business like the smartest
one, a female as the poems say
she got him and she slew him, he was that far gone
he couldn't leave off, she was so much his poison
so much his dish, he'd turn on a dime
to give her her wish

But the thing they didn't know
who didn't know him, was he knew how
she looked when she looked at him

And now you can see, there's a moral here.
It happened in Crete. Or if you're discreet,

I can tell you
more: it's no different, just down the street

The Lordly and Isolate Satyrs

The lordly and isolate Satyrs—look at them come in
on the left side of the beach
like a motorcycle club! And the handsomest of them,
the one who has a woman, driving that snazzy
convertible
             Wow, did you ever see even in a museum
such a collection of boddisatvahs, the way
they come up to their stop, each of them
as though it was a rudder
the way they have to sit above it
and come to a stop on it, the monumental solidity
of themselves, the Easter Island
they make of the beach, the Red-headed Men

             These are the Androgynes,
the Fathers behind the father, the Great Halves

Or as that one was, inside his pants, the Yiddish poet
a vegetarian. Or another—all in his mouth—a snarl
of the Sources. Or the one I loved most, who once,
once only, let go the pain, the night he got drunk,
and I put him to bed, and he said, Bad blood.

           Or the one who cracks and doesn't know
that what he thinks are a thousand questions are suddenly
a thousand lumps thrown up where the cloaca
again has burst: one looks into the face and exactly as suddenly
it isn't the large eyes and nose but the ridiculously small mouth
which you are looking down as one end of

             —as the Snarled Man
is a monocyte.

          Hail the ambiguous Fathers, and look closely
at them, they are the unadmitted, the club of Themselves,
weary riders, but who sit upon the landscape as the Great
Stones. And only have fun among themselves. They are
the lonely ones

Hail them, and watch out. The rest of us,
on the beach as we had previously known it, did not know
there was this left side. As they came riding in from the sea
—we did not notice them until they were already creating
the beach we had not known was there—but we assume
they came in from the sea. We assume that. We don't know.

In any case the whole sea was now a hemisphere,
and our eyes like half a fly's, we saw twice as much. Every-
thing opened, even if the newcomers just sat, didn't,
for an instant, pay us any attention. We were as we had been,
in that respect. We were as usual, the children were being fed pop
and potato chips, and everyone was sprawled as people are
on a beach. Something had happened but the change
wasn't at all evident. A few drops of rain
would have made more of a disturbance.

There we were. They, in occupation of the whole view
in front of us and off to the left where we were not used to look.
And we, watching them pant from their exertions, and talk to each other,
the one in the convertible the only one who seemed to be circulating.
And he was dressed in magnificent clothes, and the woman with him
a dazzling blond, the new dye making her hair a delicious
streaked ash. She was as distant as the others. She sat in her flesh too.

These are our counterparts, the unknown ones.

They are here. We do not look upon them as invaders. Dimensionally

they are larger than we—all but the woman. But we are not suddenly

small. We are as we are. We don't even move, on the beach.

It is a stasis. Across nothing at all we stare at them.
We can see what they are. They don't notice us. They have merely
and suddenly moved in. They occupy our view. They are between us
and the ocean. And they have given us a whole new half of beach.

As of this moment, there is nothing else to report.
It is Easter Island transplanted to us. With the sun, and a warm
summer day, and sails out on the harbor they're here, the Con-
temporaries. They have come in.

Except for the stirring of the leader, they are still
catching their breath. They are almost like scooters the way
they sit there, up a little, on their thing. It is as though
the extra effort of it tired them the most. Yet that just there
was where their weight and separateness—their immensities—

lay. Why they seem like boddisatvahs. The only thing one noticed
is the way their face breaks when they call across to each other.
Or actually speak quite quietly, not wasting breath. But the face
loses all containment, they are fifteen year old boys at the moment
they speak to each other. They are not gods. They are not even stone.
They are doubles. They are only Source. When they act like us
they go to pieces. One notices then that their skin
is only creased like red-neck farmers. And that they are all
freckled. The red-headed people have the hardest time
to possess themselves. Is it because they were over-
fired? Or why—even to their beautiful women—do the red ones
have only that half of the weight?

        We look at them, and begin to know. We begin to see
who they are. We see why they are satyrs, and why one half
of the beach was unknown to us. And now that it is known,
now that the beach goes all the way to the headland we thought
we were huddling ourselves up against, it turns out it is the
same. It is beach. The Visitors—Resters—who, by being there,
made manifest what we had not known—that the beach fronted wholly
to the sea—have only done that, completed the beach.

        The difference is
we are more on it. The beauty of the white of the sun's light, the
blue the water is, and the sky, the movement on the painted lands-
cape, the boy-town the scene was, is now pierced with angels and
with fire. And winter's ice shall be as brilliant in its time as
life truly is, as Nature is only the offerer, and it is we
who look to see what the beauty is.

        These visitors, now stirring
to advance, to go on wherever they do go restlessly never completing
their tour, going off on their motorcycles, each alone except for
the handsome one, isolate huge creatures wearing down nothing as
they go, their huge third leg like carborundum, only the vault
of their being taking rest, the awkward boddhas

        We stay. And watch them
gather themselves up. We have no feeling except love. They are not
ours. They are of another name. These are what the gods are. They
look like us. They are only in all parts larger. But the size is
only different. The difference is, they are not here, they are not
on this beach in this sun which, tomorrow, when we come to swim,
will be another summer day. They can't talk to us. We have no desire
to stop them any more than, as they made their camp, only possibly
the woman in the convertible one might have wanted to be familiar
with. The Leader was too much as they.

        They go. And the day

A Newly Discovered 'Homeric' Hymn

(for Jane Harrison, if she were alive)

Hail and beware the dead who will talk life until you are blue
in the face. And you will not understand what is wrong,
they will not be blue, they will have tears in their eyes,
they will seem to you so much more full of life
than the rest of us, and they will ask so much, not of you no
but of life, they will cry, isn't it this way, if it isn't
I don't care for it, and you will feel the blackmail, you will not know
what to answer, it will all have become one mass

Hail and beware them, for they come from where you have not been,
they come from where you cannot have come, they come into life
by a different gate. They come from a place which is not easily known,
it is known only to those who have died. They carry seeds
you must not touch, you must not touch the pot they taste of,
no one must touch the pot, no one must, in their season.

Hail and beware them, in their season. Take care. Prepare
to receive them, they carry what the living cannot do without,
but take the proper precautions, do the prescribed things, let
down the thread from the right shoulder. And from the forehead.
And listen to what they say, listen to the talk, hear
every word of it—they are drunk from the pot, they speak
like no living man may speak, they have the seeds in their mouth—
listen, and beware

Hail them solely that they have the seeds in their mouth, they
are drunk, you cannot do without a drunkenness, seeds can't
they must be soaked in the contents of the pot, they must be all one mass.
But you who live cannot know what else the seeds must be. Hail
and beware the earth, where the dead come from. Life
is not of the earth. The dead are of the earth. Hail and beware
the earth, where the pot is buried.

Greet the dead in the dead man's time. He is drunk of the pot.
He speaks like spring does. He will deceive you. You are meant
to be deceived. You must observe the drunkenness. You are not to
drink. But you must hear, and see. You must beware.

Hail them, and fall off. Fall off! The drink is not yours,
it is not yours! You do not come
from the same place, you do not suffer as the dead do,
they do not suffer, they need, because they have drunk of the pot,
they need. Do not drink of the pot, do not touch it. Do not touch
them.

   Beware the dead. And hail them. They teach you drunkenness.
You have your own place to drink. Hail and beware them, when they come.

As the Dead Prey Upon Us

As the dead prey upon us,
they are the dead in ourselves,
awake, my sleeping ones, I cry out to you,
disentangle the nets of being!

I pushed my car, it had been sitting so long unused.
I thought the tires looked as though they only needed air.
But suddenly the huge underbody was above me, and the rear tires
were masses of rubber and thread variously clinging together

as were the dead souls in the living room, gathered
about my mother, some of them taking care to pass
beneath the beam of the movie projector, some record
playing on the victrola, and all of them
desperate with the tawdriness of their life in hell

I turned to the young man on my right and asked, "How is it,
there?" And he begged me protestingly don't ask, we are poor
poor. And the whole room was suddenly posters and presentations
of brake linings and other automotive accessories, cardboard
displays, the dead roaming from one to another
as bored in life as they are in hell, poor and doomed
to mere equipments.

            my mother, as alive as ever she was, asleep
when I entered the house as I often found her in a rocker
under the lamp, and awaking, as I came up to her, as she ever had

I found out she returns to the house once a week, and with her
the throng of the unknown young who enter on her as much in death
as other like suited and dressed people did in life

O the dead!

        and the Indian woman and I
        enabled the blue deer
        to walk

and the blue deer talked,
in the next room,
a Negro talk

it was like walking a jackass,
and its talk
was the pressing gabber of gammers
of old women

and we helped walk it around the room
because it was seeking socks
or shoes for its hooves
now that it was acquiring

human possibilities

In the five hindrances men and angels
stay caught in the net, in the immense nets
which spread out across each plane of being, the multiple nets
which hamper at each step of the ladders as the angels
and the demons
and men
go up and down

      Walk the jackass
      Hear the victrola
      Let the automobile
      be tucked into a corner of the white fence
      when it is a white chair. Purity

is only an instant of being, the trammels

recur

In the five hindrances, perfection
is hidden
      I shall get
      to the place
      10 minutes late.

      It will be 20 minutes
      of 9. And I don't know,

      without the car,

      how I shall get there

O peace, my mother, I do not know
how differently I could have done
what I did or did not do.

        That you are back each week
        that you fall asleep
        with your face to the right

        that you are as present there
        when I come in as you were
        when you were alive

        that you are as solid, and your flesh
        is as I knew it, that you have the company
        I am used to your having

        but o, that you all find it
        such a cheapness!

o peace, mother, for the mammothness
of the comings and goings
of the ladders of life

The nets we are entangled in. Awake,
my soul, let the power into the last wrinkle
of being, let none of the threads and rubber of the tires
be left upon the earth. Let even your mother
go. Let there be only paradise

The desperateness is, that the instant
which is also paradise (paradise
 is happiness) dissolves
into the next instant, and power
flows to meet the next occurrence

        Is it any wonder
        my mother comes back?
        Do not that throng
        rightly seek the room
        where they might expect
        happiness? They did not complain
        of life, they obviously wanted
        the movie, each other, merely to pass
        among each other there,
        where the real is, even to the display cards,
        to be out of hell

The poverty
of hell

O souls, in life and in death,
awake, even as you sleep, even in sleep
know what wind
even under the crankcase of the ugly automobile
lifts it away, clears the sodden weights of goods,
equipment, entertainment, the foods the Indian woman,
the filthy blue deer, the 4 by 3 foot 'Viewbook,'
the heaviness of the old house, the stuffed inner room
lifts the sodden nets

       and they disappear as ghosts do,
       as spider webs, nothing
       before the hand of man

       The vent! You must have the vent,
       or you shall die. Which means
       never to die, the ghastliness

       of going, and forever
       coming back, returning
       to the instants which were not lived

       O mother, this I could not have done,
       I could not have lived what you didn't,
       I am myself netted in my own being

       I want to die. I want to make that instant, too,
       perfect

       O my soul, slip
       the cog

II

The death in life (death itself)
is endless, eternity
is the false cause

The knot is other wise, each topological corner
presents itself, and no sword
cuts it, each knot is itself its fire

each knot of which the net is made
is for the hands to untake
and knot's making. And touch alone

can turn the knot into its own flame

          (o mother, if you had once touched me

          o mother, if I had once touched you)

The car did not burn. Its underside
was not presented to me
a grotesque corpse. The old man

merely removed it as I looked up at it,
and put it in a corner of the picket fence
like was it my mother's white dog?

or a child's chair

          The woman,
          playing on the grass,
          with her son (the woman next door)

          was angry with me whatever it was
          slipped across the playpen or whatever
          she had out there on the grass

          And I was quite flip in reply
          that anyone who used plastic
          had to expect things to skid

          and break, that I couldn't worry
          that her son might have been hurt
          by whatever it was I sent skidding

          down on them.

          It was just then I went into my house
          and to my utter astonishment
          found my mother sitting there

          as she always had sat, as must she always
          forever sit there her head lolling
          into sleep? Awake, awake my mother

          what wind will lift you too
          forever from the tawdriness,
          make you rich as all those souls

          crave crave crave

to be rich?

They are right. We must have
what we want. We cannot afford
not to. We have only one course:

the nets which entangle us are flames

        O souls, burn
        alive, burn now

        that you may forever
        have peace, have

        what you crave

        O souls,
        go into everything,
        let not one knot pass
        through your fingers

        let not any they tell you
        you must sleep as the net
        comes through your authentic hands

        What passes
        is what is, what shall be, what has
        been, what hell and heaven is
        is earth to be rent, to shoot you
        through the screen of flame which each knot
        hides as all knots are a wall ready
        to be shot open by you

                        the nets of being
        are only eternal if you sleep as your hands
        ought to be busy. Method, method

        I too call on you to come
        to the aid of all men, to women most
        who know most, to woman to tell
        men to awake. Awake, men,
        awake

I ask my mother
to sleep. I ask her
to stay in the chair.

My chair
is in the corner of the fence.
She sits by the fireplace made of paving stones. The blue deer
need not trouble either of us.

And if she sits in happiness the souls
who trouble her and me
will also rest. The automobile

has been hauled away.

Moonset, Gloucester,
December 1, 1957, 1:58 AM

Goodbye red moon
In that color you set
west of the Cut I should imagine
forever Mother

After 47 years this month
a Monday at 9 AM
you set I rise I hope
a free thing as probably
what you more were Not
the suffering one you sold
sowed me on Rise
Mother from off me
God damn you God damn me my
misunderstanding of you

I can die now I just begun to live

Borne down by the inability to lift the heaviness,
            and Zeus walks off with Ganymede smiling

My eyes down cast while talking at too much distance
from my friend,
            and Zeus walks on, and off with Ganymede

The days all the fall of the year and man and woman calling
for a new deal,

            and there Zeus is with his fillet tilted and the tilt
            in his eye,

            and he comes right through, snatching
            the boy as he goes

How light I am if I thought of it and hot
if I were inside one foot distance

            And the boy lets him, gaily
            with a lock falling on his captor's shoulder

            and still holding the cock he had, Ganymede
            lets Zeus walk off with him, smiling

The Company of Men

for Phil Whalen for Christmas 1957

               both, the company of men,
one, in front of my eyes, bringing in red fish, the other
the far-flung East India Company of poets whom I do not
even know

tons of fish against which to assert pinholes (I punch
the music I want out on rolls of paper to be played on
anyone's parlor harmonium   (the particles
of speech as multiple as those dull repeating patterns
of fish (nature runs to pattern; man, said Lawrence,
cannot afford to repeat

         I mean the finances
         of men (who gave us a haddock

         True Numbers
         are the usableness (how fishermen

         pay their bills. The catch

         repeats but the generosity
         can come only

         from those
         who have fish

In the company of men
what jingles

in his pocket
on Main Street

              The South Sea
              or Oaxaca

              is a Bubble (what blew

              John Law, why Campion

kicked rhyme in the face: Humphreys
has resigned knowing

the nation
will go boom

I mean Phil
Whalen

who brings his girl
a stalk

torn off
a rhododendron

in the public
park

Or my dragger
who goes home with

arete: when his wife
complains he smells like

his Aunt who works
for the De-Hy

he whips out
his pay

and says, how does this
smell?

The Distances

So the distances are Galatea
                            and one does fall in love and desires
mastery
                   old Zeus—young Augustus

Love knows no distance, no place
                         is that far away or heat changes
into signals, and control
                   old Zeus—young Augustus

Death is a loving matter, then, a horror
                         we cannot bide, and avoid
by greedy life
           we think all living things are precious
           —Pygmalions

                         a German inventor in Key West
who had a Cuban girl, and kept her, after her death
in his bed
                       after her family retrieved her
he stole the body again from the vault

Torso on torso in either direction,
             young Augustus
                        out via nothing where messages
are
     or in, down La Cluny's steps to the old man sitting
a god throned on torsoes,
           old Zeus

Sons go there hopefully as though there was a secret, the object
to undo distance?
                      They huddle there, at the bottom
of the shaft, against one young bum
                 or two loving cheeks,
         Augustus?

You can teach the young nothing
                        all of them go away, Aphrodite
tricks it out,
            old Zeus—young Augustus

You have love, and no object
                        or you have all pressed to your nose
which is too close,
            old Zeus hiding in your chin your young
            Galatea

the girl who makes you weep, and you keep the corpse live by all
your arts
            whose cheek do you stroke when you stroke the stone face
            of young Augustus, made for bed in a military camp,
            o Caesar?

O love who places all where each is, as they are, for every moment,
yield
            to this man
                        that the impossible distance
be healed,
            that young Augustus
            and old Zeus
be enclosed

            "I wake you,
stone. Love this man."

(Descensus spiritus, No. 1)

She who hits at will

with dog and catalpa, panicles
streaked
yellow and brown purple, she

was treetops, we floated
entwined, she tossed
her blossoms while below

her dog floated
in the Hudson, precious to her and I was surprised
she had a dog

I said her, the flower
and the dog are equal, equalized
as creations of you, you snow, you are streaked, you

gentlest water

The year is a great circle or
the year is a great mistake

Capricorn (of sizable thirst)
stumbles up first—cold dry street, with ladies, and night

shoves aside the year (Boob of the movable cardinal and not melancholic
daylight) bears on his back an ass and the exaltation
of wars

He and his son and his son's son (Water Boy)
butt their way in and out of every
place of creation. They're all
knees

In a sort of reverse apocatastasis, that is, the tail's
where the head ought to be, these
Long Ears

though being locked up does not prove
(they missed the stakeout to bag junkeys)
they don't shove. They shove

all all directions

The Red Fish-of-Bones

The Red Fish-of-Bones
the Blue Fish
& the White Fish

the eye of the Red Fish of Bones
the quick soft turning & yearning of the White Fish
toward the Red Fish of Bones,

tied as she is
to the Blue Fish who comes
over so fast to interfere

places himself majestically
between the Red Fish of Bones
& his lady.

But the Red Fish of Bones
swings the swing binds
the White Fish to the majestic

Blue Fish of Bones
and swinging wide suddenly
the consort, the White Fish of Bones

is back between
the Red Fish of Bones
and the Blue

& the three
swim in the air peacefully
again.

But for a moment
only—the Blue
Fish of the Air

swims in directly
to the eye of the
Red Fish of Bones

and the White consort
is again off alone like the moon
with Venus.

So forever they jockey
in their three estates,
the Red Fish of the Bones

with his eye for her,
the Blue Fish with her
on the same string,

& she in the middle the winsome
wife, caught in her turning
& maybe her yearning

by the Red Fish of the Bones
whose power over each
is not sufficient

against the Blue Fish of the Bones'
majesty, to bring the White Fish Lady
over across from

the delicate turning of all
in the everlasting air
of the currents

which turn
the Red Fish of the Bones
the White Fish and the Blue Fish

together in turning
and in her yearning
if it is yearning

bound to the Blue Fish
but looking
out from under his majestical turning,

at the eye
of the Red Fish turning, in his sweep,
them both but not reaching

her delicate turning,
the White Fish
of the Bones

of Women

WHITE HANDS
(or the ladies'
white legs—*no*
distress LEFT

   This magic
   is not for, or for only,
   the PRIESTS

The Americans

the cosmologist says
what constitutes a society:
an assemblage of atoms
makes the thing go

why the social stinks
—and each American stinks—
is that it is an inadequate
number of cells they are
sitting in a room,
to constitute an organism

they aren't cooked
and ruled by information

turn now and rise

Wrest the matter into your own

hands—and Nature's laws

Across Space and Time

If the great outside system—species and stars—proceeds
successfully across great time, and curves to return to
stations it was once in before, and the belt of the ecliptic
slides like her cestus in months of a great year taking
25,725.6 years, what wonder that any one of us may be inflamed
with love at birth and spend a lifetime seeking to take the tail
into one's mouth, the disaster or augery of the shape and voluntas
of one's person, cast out of the combinatorial, substance the real
at the moment of birth, and one's own love the affectiones to cause
all of it to swarm, to know that as those beasts wheel variously
onto the point where night and day are equal one now does approach
the date at which man will pour equally from left to right out of
the pitcher of his portion of creation?

> Hail, Aquarius,
> who is coming in

The Fish swam in on the back of Christ, by 1180 Christ was catching
the fish, by the 19th by carbon test (plus or minus 157 years) the fish
was sailing off, the Renaissance was over. Now the 2nd, and the 20th
were like (analogues) of a different source and of a different struct-
ure, presenting a small Renaissance and a great world state to rush in
to petrify the dragging years of the fish bones, limestone for a future
to come up out of the sea on, when water has again made sense out of
things

> Farewell, Fish, your bones
> we shall walk on

> Before either, Manes, the son of Sargon, swept out
> into the Atlantic while horsemen from the Caucasus
> came in with Aries to shake the dead temple world
> and awake self and reason, the soft Aries people who ride
> horses backward, brilliant riders who only know the back
> is an engine of will to be sacrificed if the sons
> will have wives, they ride on into battle until al'
> is divided between flesh and soul and Greece
> is the measure of what they were worth

Ram long gone,
you won't come back
You are hopelessly torn
by the heels of the bulls

America, you are the end of three months of man. For the third,
which began when your head was turned, already has changed you,
you nation of Finks. Let you rule the world. You are a dead hand.
Man, in his courses, is on the other side: Capricorn is drawing
the threads

The Allegory of Wealth

a Poem from America still

On the other phone, Persephone: 'He crushed me,—he creased my britches,'

and the load, of the Fatman, on a body, the thought
of the bones broken in a body by weight, not by a blow,
crushed. And then, the life goes, the cry, in her voice. My soul

and I rushed to go across the space from one skyscraper office
to the other, to try to help, to see if there was anything
one might do, what the Milliardaire had done to the Maid.

The Librarian

The landscape (the landscape!) again: Gloucester,
the shore one of me is (duplicates), and from which
(from offshore, I, Maximus) am removed, observe.

In this night I moved on the territory with combinations
(new mixtures) of old and known personages: the leader,
my father, in an old guise, here selling books and manuscripts.

My thought was, as I looked in the window of his shop,
there should be materials here for Maximus, when, then,
I saw he was the young musician has been there (been before me)

before. It turned out it wasn't a shop, it was a loft (wharf-
house) in which, as he walked me around, a year ago
came back (I had been there before, with my wife and son,

I didn't remember, he presented me insinuations via
himself and his girl) both of whom I had known for years.
But never in Gloucester. I had moved them in, to my country.

His previous appearance had been in my parents' bedroom where I
found him intimate with my former wife: this boy
was now the Librarian of Gloucester, Massachusetts!

> Black space,
> old fish–house.
> Motions
> of ghosts.
> I,
> dogging
> his steps.
>
> He
> (not my father,
> by name himself
> with his face
> twisted
> at birth)

possessed of knowledge
pretentious
giving me
what in the instant
I knew better of.

But the somber
place, the flooring
crude like a wharf's
and a barn's
space

I was struck by the fact I was in Gloucester, and that my daughter
was there—that I would see her! She was over the Cut. I
hadn't even connected her with my being there, that she was

here. That she was there (in the Promised Land—the Cut!
But there was this business, of poets, that all my Jews
were in the fish-house too, that the Librarian had made a party

I was to read. They were. There were many of them, slumped
around. It was not for me. I was outside. It was the Fort.
The Fort was in East Gloucester—old Gorton's Wharf, where the Library

was. It was a region of coal houses, bins. In one a gang
was beating someone to death, in a corner of the labyrinth
of fences. I could see their arms and shoulders whacking

down. But not the victim. I got out of there. But cops
tailed me along the Fort beach toward the Tavern

The places still
half-dark, mud,
coal dust.

There is no light
east
of the Bridge

Only on the headland
toward the harbor
from Cressy's

have I seen it (once
when my daughter ran
out on a spit of sand

isn't even there.) Where
is Bristow? when does I-A
get me home? I am caught

in Gloucester. (What's buried
behind Lufkin's
Diner? Who is

Frank Moore?

abt the dead he sd
he was going to write an obit
about those americans, dead,
who had shaped the world, he sd,
with a more than heavy hand

                now she sd, looking up
                at the bomb like it was a bird
                got between her
                and the sun

                        I don't know
                what she sd about Grant
                Phil Whalen
                insisted
                San Francisco
                1957
                that everything I ever sd
                she sd But abt Grant

                I sd Butcher I read
                Kenneth Williams
                on Grant I feel Grant
                more days in more
                of those fall-ins
                where the glue, it feels,
                of the creation is all
                that holds anything
                back?

                The next turn of the wheel,
                what do you think
                about the next turn
                of the wheel?

The Binnacle

The binnacle! the
binnacle—the smallest
fluid in
the ocean: who floats
in what, thus

lends it di-
rection. What sticks
moves, within as
in the world-
ocean, we offer

considerable
resistance, men
and women making
the wind rose (sitted in
the points, not

loxodromes!) Eyes,
& lines. The gy-
res-
copes (a
        continuously driven, whose
spinning is,
so that the earth's
causes it (us) to
point
        (a wheel or disk mounted
         but also free to,

and to any torque which
would try

us

2

Each makes room for itself
and rhumb lines as it moves

Place; & Names

a place as term in the order of creation
& thus useful as a function of that equation
example, that the "Place Where the Horse-Sacrificers Go"
of the Brihadaranyaka Upanishad is worth more than
a metropolis—or, for that matter, any moral
concept, even a metaphysical one
                                    and that this is so
for physical & experimental reasons of
the *philosphia perennis,* or Isness
of cosmos beyond those philosophies
or religious or moral systems of
rule, thus giving factors of naming
—nominative power—& landschaft
experience (geography) which stay truer
to space-time than personalities
or biographies of such terms as specific
cities or persons, as well as the inadequacy
to the order of creation of anything except
names—including possibly mathematics (?)

the crucialness being that these places or names
be as parts of the body, common, & capable
therefore of having cells which can decant
total experience—no selection
other than one which is capable
of this commonness (permanently
duplicating) will work

"Story" in other words is if not superior
at least equal to ultimate mathematical
language—perhaps superior because of
cell-ness (?) In any case history
(as to be understood by Duncan's Law
to mean a) histology & b) story)
applies here, in this equational way
& severely at the complementarity of
cosmos (complementary to individual
or private) and not to cities or
events in the way it has, in
a mistaken secondary way, been
understood

I've been absorbed by the subject of America all my life. One piece of it has been what the enclosed hopes, in that sense, to set down. Actually as in fact it was reading and playing it out as a child in redoubts we imagined trenches and trees on the foot of Fisher's Hill we were sure had been a part of earlier Indian wars the books of James Altschuler —and I am now convinced there are indeed only "three" American stories—that which was 1st, the one Cowpens actualized (the "line" which the Proclamation of 1763 made the Appalachian Ridge)—and then the West. So I *have* here a much larger story than would appear.

Charles Olson 1966

as of Bozeman

Red Cloud (DAB) succeeded
left conf. Laramie 1866 June
& for two years, inc. Fetterman
massacre (Dec 1866) &
at the Wagon Box fight (Aug
1867 (also attack on Hayfield
party near Fort C.F. Smith)
he won: govt, by treaty of 1868,
closed trail & 3 forts abandoned

2nd. Ann.
cf. Report of Board of Indian
    Commissioners 1870 (1871)
on visit to Washington

---

for biblio, cf. next page—
was chief of the Oglalas, the
largest tribe of the Teton Sioux
father: Lone Man; mother: Walks as
                        She Thinks

At same time also investigate
Red Cloud's friendship with
    Othniel C. Marsh, Am.
    paleontolgist (see DAB)

(all by
        W. J. Ghent (?)

Was the Bozeman Rd to the gold
fields of Montana??
                (cf Ghent
            on Spotted Tail)

Gold disc. Black Hills 1874

———————————

Bozeman fr Georgia—gold seeker

Crazy Horse

(1849–1877
28!

Two Poems

men are only known in memory
Red Cloud's mind invested Fort Phil Kearny
and produced the careful form of Fetterman's
troop's dispersion upon the landscape of
those rounded hills creating the area
on which he left their parts, and caps
and uniforms and designed thereby
any other event such as (with Crazy Horse
was it in command Yellow Horse Young
Bull) the removal of Custer and
his several persons in an easy
lay-out. There isn't (after the small
incitement of the scene those yards
was it almost out from the Fort on
Bozeman's gold road) any longer,
thereafter, a connection to agricultural
time. Grant as a supplier and his
Southern counterpart's extraordinary ability
to disengage—one with Washington
as his personal mold the other with none
and so more raw to war, neither Indian
nor inheritor of a measure to abide by
U S Grant is a spasm of time
                              (Apr,
                              (LXIII)

The Pedens, who re-walked the trails, hobbyists
or their own model & predecessor who re-walked from Salt
Lake—or then one jumps to DeVoto hauling & lowering
teams up over & down from the Wasatch Range
where the difficulties for the Donners ate 'em like the bites
of the bug which got 'em soon enough, poor
World Travelers of the late
New World, the assembláge

of Californiay—there was only one way
in any way to arrive where the West was when
she had run out was by sea around or
if German in entourage like observers and watercolorists,
of the Civil War: Port Orford or the slash
country back of it until you get east enough to the comfort
away from the brutalization of the Pacific
Orford is a peninsula none try but Cyclops
who are themselves nothing but caked-eyes
like Salt Lake north where Fitzpatrick crossed
on his mule & with his Indian wife frightful
places lie passively in Edons on Pacifica
no good yet hubris and hybrids or eyelids
against bad light no hope for Sutter slicked
Doner only Sauer—and Duncan who trot-mocs
in with the light of seance and the golden light
of those paintings he knows what the dream
may be carries a fowling piece like the possible
World Travelers imagine Duncan in doe-skin
and with his fowling piece—between
those romantic paintings and not Peter Rabbit Robert
Duncan in fringed jacket against the bad sunset
from all across the intermediary space,
                                        the East

doesn't get home beyond
Sacramento

Drummond Hadley

TWO POEMS

THE RANGE

What these sounds were
there among the rocks and trees
when I did not know
in the mountains,
and while I came down
and asked of them,
they stayed
and returned out of me,
to the places
where they had been.

PSYCHE

that each object knew the way for Psyche
as if it were a part of way itself,
her self a tower into sky
and Tartarus which led her there.
What she was before
this winged creature is not known.
She must have lain
as though in the wet earth
she were a place of cave,
before what was within her.

Soul, and Psyche, and Animus (Will
: a man's life to be a continual
Allegory
              all which is and happens,
that one brings about, crushing
like a herd of frightened elephant anything
under foot, passing as I did
on the back of the Elephant altogether puzzling
to me how we did go between trees through
everything as a will passed through any obstacle
he was as anagogic visions in his power to
pass,
        the Elephant
on whose back I also was slim

West 6

probably the most important person I met in Vancouver
—and the most important
conversation
and event
                    so many miles
up over the Pacific Ocean
        looking down on
        whether those were coots
        or sea gulls
        in
        the evening
        water

        Coolidges present too
        and Rosemary
        Margaret
        did not walk out
        (why not?)

                and Diana Hadley
        gave me her pink sweater

    as I also was wearing Drummond Hadley's
        trench coat (?)

(and who read that night
was it Duncan?)

            that marge
    of the few feet make the difference
    between the West, and the Future
Robin Blaser,
and Duncan,
and that dream

at the same time as I was writing
about the distance
between Sacramento
and the old old West

Robin Blaser and Mountain Meadow Massacre

one lone Indian
fishing in the river at the bottom of
the Barranca del cobre

charles olson, March 4
(XIX-LXIV

To Empty the Mind

                    the gracious gods
                    the red man
                    and the white man
                    how deliberately Sam Adams parlayed
                    the "Battle of Lexington" as he had
                    previously set up the Boston
                    Massacre as well as led his Mohawks
                    out of Fanuel Hall to bring about
                    the Boston Tea Party—failing to get a Constitutional
                    Army

                    and that the Reverend Jonas Clarke
                    in whose house the plot was laid
                    talked John Locke freshly
                    during the night thus adding
                    these general ideas:

at 1 :30 AM the militiamen's own decision
was not to meddle with the British soldiers
coming down the pike

                    to leave us
                    to our concerns
                    thus were the parts
                    of all the parts of the bodies
                    of the Federal Cavalry troop
                    —Lieut. Fetterman's command—left around
                    the landscape on and about the dun hills by
                    Fort Phil Kearny

(for Ed Dorn

Oh! fa-doo : the enormous success of clerks
due to the even greater success of Agency men

Oh! for a man because myself have seen his demeanor
no less civil than he excellent in the quality he professes!

besides divers of worship (Gentlemen) have reported
his uprightness of dealing, which argues his honesty,

—and his facetious grace in writing that approves his art"

Oh! the Beauty who had his Heart wrapped in a Woman's Hide!

—An anonymous contributor from
Wyoming, New York.

A Note for Anyone Able to

> I cldn't advise you than to study more the
> 13th century   especially the 1st half
> & particularly the contrast (4th Century Athens!)
> of the 2nd Half

'Outis

pitcher, how
exactly is
the feeling of the threads
what it is—that is,
the drama we know about,
the g(love)

or how is bush league bush
(man) made major, made
to bear in, to bear
down? in what sense is
to hit long before the ball
reaches
whoever?

where does giddiness
where is it
ceased—how can you say how
you can be said to be
cool, can throw it
exactly as how the ball is, how
you be sd to hurl?

(again): the whirl
is very much exaggerated, the
crowd, the afternoon, and, even,
the exhilaration of the home
run, though the centerfield wall
—to point at it—is exactly
a like term, is also
as you pitch

that is, as of a day, a
double day, say, as this, when
there is a crowd, how would you say
how far back you are reaching from
say, big train, from, the dirt, in what way
do you obey
the given, the
taken—how much grip
do your fingers have
on those threads, or.
for that matter,
the hide, eh?

Memory, Mind, and Will
: politics,

make money
& assert
yourself use
public service use
the citizen carry out
public policy sell
your ideas to the tax payer and
you can vote in America without paying
any taxes viz
there are men with ideas
who effect

public policy via
politicians including
leaders of service unions
who can tie up distribution

there is size
to Union
which is different
than size or
more of same, either of which

in the present state of these States
are no longer as interesting as

the admission of politics

for Ed Dorn, and with kudos
for Leroi Jones

Buffalo Ode

Section 1

As Sir Saltonstall ran over
the Atlantic waves carrying the virus
cut down Arbella Lincoln,

and out on the Western plains Bill Gratwyck
the First, skidded into a stop
at Lake Erie's shore almost burning
his hooves off when the rail
ran into the end of the land,

Tycoonery had a wedding in 1904

Section 2

the Holland Land Grant troubled no one, wolves' pelts drew
5 £ up through 1830, and so one does have to look
at Dutch American History as prior and conceivably equal
in social power swung onto International Affairs
at a date enough to raise two important questions:
the investment of the Hudson Valley
wo do know all about but exactly what the teaching
of wampum value to the Pilgrim Fathers does betoken
of earlier sea-coast venturing by Dutch maritime knowledges
let us look in J G Ryans or Mahoney's Documents of Early New York History
to determine what it did mean to begin this Empire State

Section 3

a dog with a head at each end
the Erie Canal made New York State

and Dutch patroons refused
what Philadelphias had to do

       the Albany men had such a good deal
       up north at Montreal

so it was proper by William Jennings Bryan
for William Gratwyck I
to fly in here by jet
and propell Niagara power
in railroad even maybe shredded wheat
to make the new end of the dog
be head as at the other end
of Hudson River was the city
which even then had not
become Metropolis

draw the lines the Master said

Section 4

and Massachusetts men sold Dutchmen via Robert Morris
the go of infested Genesee and mouth of Buffalo
Creek where Senecas had been pushed until
Transit Road was the line of future Democratic Power
on this end of the dog Paul Fitzpatrick State Committee Boss because
Buffalo was worth the State's electoral vote by cancelling
the Finger Lakes and so forth all through the middle of the State

     from Chatauqua country on
     to the Bronx line

Connecticut farm houses dotting
     with Greco-Roman elegance
     right out of Asher Benjamin's
     builders book and gingerbread
     and Victorian as good until
       1904

Section 5

New York City was the mart of the State
until the crookedness of the telegraph
reporting the sway
of the losses at Antietam
allowed
such men as Daniel Drew
to make money directly out of blood

previous to that moment he like the Astors
had been butchers or drivers literally of meat
to feed the city originally
from the hills of Conneticut or Vermont down then
from Upper New York State via Fodham Road where Drew
invented watered stock by filling his cattle by
giving them salt and then
he went to the Pennsylvania and there
the Allegheny West went open: Cowpens
of the Mountain Ranges

a piece of the song of the white men

up Lansing went, to Chagrin Falls
just far enough from the Hudson
to go all the way, the chaise

the choice out of 28
      on any New York estate

a piece of the song of the Indians–and the white men

Cowpens–and Gurty, Doones and
Double men all holed up, at
Indian Town, New York: from
New Haven etc and Brant
and Johnson as the French
had whacked the town, to shake it
loose, to get it off
the Indian and White man's
back-country, the
City-Without, the Hole-in-the-Scheme, the Refuse-
Refuge, the 'Paris'-Sewer, the
        Otsego

you can't use words as ideas any more than that they can be strung
as sounds. They are meanings only and actions of their own sort

      feeling and desires and breath
the cause of the words coming into existence
ahead of them, the nose bringing them out ahead of its—
self, and a principle, their own meaning, enough
animus so it all has
will

Feminine
Writing so that all the World
is redeemed, and history
and all that politics,
and "State" and Subjection
are for once, done away with,
  as the reason
of writing

The Grandfather-Father Poem

rolled in the grass
like an overrun horse
or a poor dog
to cool himself
from his employment
in the South Works
of U S Steel
as an Irish shoveler

    to make their fires hot
    to make ingots above
    by puddlers of
    melted metal

    and my grandfather
    down below
    at the bottom of the
    rung

    stoking
their furnaces
with black
soft
coal soft coal
makes fire
heat higher
sooner,
        beloved
Jack Hines (whose picture
in a devil's
cap—black jack
Hines

    and would come home
   to the little white house
   sitting by itself
   on Mitchell Street
       or was then

Middle River Road
and take off
all his clothes, down to
his full red underwear
the way the story was told

and go out there
on the grass
and roll
and roll

            my
            grandfather

            my Jack Hines
            whose picture
            I have lost

I have also lost
the tin-type
of—was it?—my mother's
mother? a severe face
tight actually

her cheeks
colored false pink
nothing like the
limber
of that harsh
grandfather's
face in the picture

            loving man
            who hated

my father, would
understand
anyone

            and go stupid
when attacked by like
Irish blockheads to
what also conceivable my
grandfather may
have been gave allegiances to
—like the Church I don't know

                    was a whiskey
                        drinker
                    but no drunk

                            stored barrels
                                of apples
                            in his cellar
                                        etc

        there was nothing
            that I can honestly recall
        wasn't
        'strict' about him—that is he wasn't
        soft, I don't believe. He would my impression is give up
        anything to
        anyone or any
        thing: (impossible to be

        accurate about
        'memories' in
        that generation
        unless

            like one's own parents
        they live long enough
            for you yourself
            to be able to

        judge: on my father
        I'm afraid I am
        right, that he did fight
        rigidly the next generation of
        'Irish' in the
        U S Post Office to

                mon grand
                Père: Paddy Hehir
                    "Blocky" Sheehan
                and the Postmaster,
                Healy, ran a travel agency
                    Pleasant Street
                            Worcester

        killed himself
        'fighting'

such men (when my grandfather
rolled right over on the rug
when he was leaning over the window seat
getting some magazine say out of the inside
(with the cushions off) when I
came up from behind
and kicked him

      and I went out in the kitchen
  and sd to my mother Grandpa
    is lying on the floor

    he looked out of the tintype
  like a different type
than my pa

     black walnut
the bed was made of
he put the ridges in
where he missed
when he was giving
my uncle a beating

     my mother used to beg
   to be beaten
   instead

   who knows?
but I make Jack Hines
too mean
  a man and a woman either is only a thing when each
is full of blood

     This is my poem to my grandfather,

      John Hines his name was

      he migrated to the United States

      from Ireland sometime

      (my mother was born

      on this side 1872)

      before

1872

and was employed

so far as I know only

in his lifetime

on this side by

the U S Steel (retired

as such a night watchman

        after (I suppose) having

        shoveled coal most

        of his life

        He had been born "in Cork,
                brought up
       in Galway," and recently
       I figured out he must have been

sent 'home' to
Galway during
the potato famine

(the Hines,
as an Irish clan
were reasonably small
and had their center
around Gort

The Lamp

you can hurry the pictures toward you but
there is that point that the whole thing itself
may be a passage, and that your own ability
may be a factor in time, in fact that
only if there is a coincidence of yourself
& the universe is there then in fact
an event. Otherwise—and surely here the cinema
is large—the auditorium can be showing
all the time. But the question is
how you yourself are doing, if you in fact
are equal, in the sense that as *a like power*
you also are there when the lights
go on. This wld seem to be a
matter of creation, not simply
the obvious matter, creation
itself. Who in fact is any of us
to be there at all? That's what
swings the matter, also—
the beam hanging from

like a foldout

---

as against a bas-
relief. No
relief no
eternity no
story no

Transcendence—the ideal

in the occurrence without any raising
of the issue. Or
the person: the Veil of each
undone.
By what is done. Follow me,
said Epimenides

Said Epimenides

Light is not color, color is not sign.
Color is not social, color is not recognition. Color
is the evidence of truth

it is a very trustworthy thing,
color

Color is the Fruits
or the Four Rivers of Paradise

—William Dorn, 1597

Color is reflective (the opposite of primary

Color should come from somewhere

It follows. It is (grammatically) demonstrative.

—WILLIAM DORN, 1597 (2)

Color is not the noun or the verb,
the subject or the action. It is
the effect. It fixes
the statement. A statement
requires it. You could not have a statement
without color.

William Dorn, 1597 (3)

'light sits under one's eyes . . .'

When I think of what Fitz Lane didn't do
painting all this light which almost
each day is enough, at least at twilight,
to rouse one as a change of air does
to the direct connection our lives bear
to the mathematic of Creation surrounding us,
I love him the more for his attempts pre-
Hawthorne to draw in silk the pinks and
umbrous hills and rocks surround
on this reflexive & reflexing
Harbor-light sits under one's eye
& being as the saucer to the in
the instance of this evening high al-
most exactly perfect half moon al-
ready going westward too

"An 'Enthusiasm'."

                Lane painted true color, and drew
                true lines, and 'view' as a prin-
                ciple he had also made true as a-
                gainst too easy (Dutch) or even a
                more brilliant landscape Turner,
                Constable (Guardi, Canalletto, Tie-
                polo even behind theirs)
What kept him 'local' or at least provincial
(and patriotic, literally, especially in his
ship scenes, and in fact his introduction of
ships into his scenes, when they weren't there
and he added them
                was rather a weakness of selection,
                some selecting necessity his principle
                of View called for if his lines and color
                were to be like it first principle
or some proposal or vision like in fact Parkman
by making France-American his subject grabbed off.

      It would be impossible to say and from my own point of view
there wasn't anything at all wrong with 'Gloucester' actually
as such a proposal (and my own experience of his paintings
and his drawings is that with the isolated exception of Castine
the contrast is his
Boston Harbor or Beacon Hill
his New York Harbor and
his Savannah and San Juan Porto Rico paintings
his Gloucesters are altogether his best. It is as though
he got as far as Parkman and Prescott and even as far as
NoahWebster (in the sense of the virtue of his colors and
line and choices of view on Gloucester & Castine—as against
Owls Head Camden Hills
      Blue Hill Soames Bay Northeast Harbor—
as establishing objects as definitions as exact today as they
were then)
             but that say
Hawthorne (born the same year) or Melville but this is larger
and Parkman is the better reference and certainly Whitman's
grab-off is far away and it may seem irrelevant for me to men-
tion it. But the thing is to be sure Lane's specificity &
"place" in exactly the Who's Who in America sense be found

out: he rates (1814–1865) only the company of the men, &
Gloucester & Castine, I have mentioned not his regional &
dull school & museum & Collectors place of "Artist" & Marine
Painter. He was one of the
chief definers of the American 'practice'—the word is
Charles Pierce's for pragmatism—which is still the con-
spicious difference of American from any other past or any
other present, no matter how much we are now almost the
true international to which all bow and acknowledge

In honor of 100th
anniversary of this loss,

Charles Olson.

A <u>Scream</u> to the Editor:

Moan the loss, another
house
is gone

      Bemoan the present
which assumes
its taste, bemoan the easiness
of smashing anything

Moan Solomon Davis'
house, gone
for the YMCA, to build another
of its cheap benevolent places
bankers raise money for,

and who loan money for new houses: each destruction doubles
our loss and doubles bankers' gain when four columns

        Bemoan a people who spend
      beyond themselves, to flourish
      and to further themselves

as well made the Solomon Davis house itself
was such George Washington
could well have been inaugurated
from its second floor,

      and now it is destroyed because 70 years ago
Gloucester already could build the Y, and Patillo's
equally ugly brick front and building

      (between them the Davis house, then 50 years old,
      was stifled squeezed in no light on one side a Patch
      of soil like a hen-yard toward Patillo's

        houses live or else why
      is *one room* in 90 Middle Street worth
      $100,000 to the Metropolitan Art Museum?

      If taste is capital of this order had not

Cape Ann Historical Scientific and Literary Society
or Cape Ann Historical Association—

if John Babson the historian *founded* both
the abovementioned society *and* the Sawyer Free Library
   —and was a banker too, and wrote, with two others, the
                      principal history
of Massachusetts banking to his time,

   how many ways can value be
   allowed to be careless with, and Hagstrom
   destroy? how many more before this obvious
   dullness shall cease?

oh city of mediocrity and cheap ambition destroying
its own shoulders its own back greedy present persons
stood upon, stop this renewing without reviewing
loss loss loss no gains oh not moan stop stop stop this

     total loss of surface and of mass,
       putting bank parking places with flowers, spaces dead so dead
   in even the sun one does not even know one passes by them
Now the capitals of Solomon Davis' house
now the second floor behind the black grill work
now the windows which reached too,

now the question who if anyone was living in it
now the vigor of the narrow and fine clapboards on the back
now that flatness right up against the street,

        one is in despair, they talk and put flowers up
      on poles high enough so no one can water them,
and nobody
objects
     when houses which have held and given light
     a century, in some cases two centuries,
                    and their flowers
     aren't even there in one month

                  —the Electric Company's
lights are there, every night, to destroy the color of color
in human faces—Main Street is as sick at night as Middle

Street is getting banker-good in sun light—a swimming pool
is now promised where Solomon Davis sat beside the Dale House
& looked with some chagrin at Sawyer's not as tasteful house
across the way,

                    I'm sick
            of caring, sick of watching
        what, known or unknown, *was* the
                ways of life . . I have no
            vested interest even in this which
            makes life.
                            Moan nothing. Hate hate hate
I hate those who take away
and do not have as good to
offer. I hate them. I hate the carelessness
            For $25,000 I do not think anyone
should ever have let the YMCA take down Solomon Davis'
house, for any purpose of the YMCA

Rocking meter
over desolation

It is worth at least pointing out
that you cannot get a shell
equal to the Mansfield house
as is. It was already
impossible for Alfred Mansfield
Brooks to do any better then
than the St. Peters Club
building when, as a young
architect. that's what he
did. It wld seem
that a city with any
pride in her be-
ing so at all wld
comprehend that
just because you can't
today build as well you'd
be advised to keep
what is itself from
dates when
one cld build. I
can recommend
architects who
are themselves modest
and aware enough to
take the following buildings and
with them as shells
& together as a
trapezoid of
order lend
back to Gloucester an
area with permanence
without at all interfering
with progress. What
in fact we have in-
stead is demolition
and service
organization. Such
is not the same as

participatory
experience. It
blinds out people into
mice. And without breath the young
without even knowing why go
anywhere to leave
what itself has no
attraction. It is
doom this City is
asking for, debris
and doom, easily.
The Moon is already
reality, in such
a mind.
My buildings are
the Gloucester Hotel
(as it was), the
next building to it up
Washington, the
Town Hall the
Brooks house itself, the
John Somes (now
Wm. Webber's etc.
But if the
Mansfield house
goes all the other
little ones on
that side are eaten
away, forever. So who,
what banker,
what organization,
is the City Council,
does the City
Manager, can the
Historical
Society—obviously
like fishing vessels the
amount of money taken
to do anything more than
eat one piece away after
another is today's
sizable calamity. This
only one man can
each man who etc
makes it at all
possible. Has Gloucester
any enough

of such like
minded per-
sons to
so effect its
own self? I
dream &
go if
no such number do
exist. Lose love
if you who live here
have not eyes to wish
for that which gone cannot
be brought back ever then
again. You shall not even miss
what you have lost. You'll only
yourself be bereft
in ignorance of what
you haven't even
known. There lies
today's claim on
this—again—one
house. A city
without a house
is already
nothing. Streets
stores & all others
living in boxes
torn from woods
on highways themselves
as dull. All
right as Kulikowski
used to say, all
right. It's yours
to lose beloved
City.

for my friend

drum upon the table you drum
the Tree of the World

drum the table you drum the point
at which communication between

Heaven, Earth, and Hell is made:

       the Tree of the World a horse
       is made,

       the Tree of the World a bow
       is

Fly up, fly out
with your ecstatic fingers

on the flat table made
of the bole of Inanna's

tree. The Tree of the World
is a voyage, the sacred

pillar. Drum
the table. Fly up fly out

just where you are. You drum the point
just where communication is made

between Heaven, Earth, and Hell. Drum
the table

who plays directly into the air

from The Song
of Ullikummi

*(translated from Hurrian and Hittite, and read at Spoleto 1965 to
honor the presence of Mr. Ezra Pound)*

fucked the Mountain
fucked her but good his mind
sprang forward
and with the rock he slept
and into her let his manhood
go five times he let it go
ten times he let it go

in ikunta luli she is three
dalugasti long
she is one and a half
palhasti wide. What below she has
up on this his mind sprang upon

When Kumarbi his wisdom
he took upon
his mind
he took his istanzani
to his piran   hattatar
istanzani   piran daskizzi

Kumarbis -za   istanzani piran hattatar
daskizzi
sticks wisdom
unto his mind   like his cock

into her
iskariskizzi

the fucking
of the Mountain
fucked the mountain   went right through it and came out
the other side

the father of all the gods
from his town Urkis
he set out
and to ikunta luli
he came

and in ikunta luli a great rock
lies
sallis perunas
kittari   he came upon
What below she has
                  he sprang upon
with his mind
           he slept
with the rock   kattan sesta
with the peruni

         and into her misikan X–natur
andan his manhood
        flowed
into her

And five times he took her
nanzankan   5-anki das
and again ten times he took her
namma man zankan   10-anki das

Arunas
the Sea

So the Norse
were neurotic
And the pre-
Hesiodic
Greeks Plus the Earliest
Irischer: one wonders
at this point then,
if neuroses like ice,
and agriculture, were
preparing
modern Non-Neurotic
Man, the
Neue Klasse of
freedom   I quote

a lady
Poet who calls herself
an Artist: no cunt
is not free, my cunt
is not free, my poetry
is my cunt, you Dirty Man you
you won't let me have my cunt because

I am free, I am an Artist, I am the
Poetry

the Heart is a clock
around which clusters
or which draws to itself
all which is the same
as itself in anything

or anyone else the
power of itself lies
all about itself in
a mathematic of feeling
which we call love

but who
love itself is the container
of all feelings otherwise than love
as well

as the heart equally
holds all else there is anywhere
in Creation, when it is
full

The intent of the following list is to record the earliest known date for each poem. Poems which are dated, either internally, or on the manuscript, have been so indicated. Poems which can be dated only approximately through references in secondary sources (letters, etc.) are indicated by 'ca.+date' or 'by+date'. The date and publisher for the first publication of each poem have been included.

Lower Field—Enniscorthy: 4/46 Harpers Monthly Magazine CXCII

A Lion upon the Floor: 1/46 Harpers Bazaar LXXX

Troilus: 8/48 Right Angle II, 5

Only the Red Fox, Only the Crow: 3/49 Atlantic Monthly CLXXXIII

Pacific Lament: 3/46 Atlantic Monthly CLXXVII

In the Hills South of Capernaum, Port: 4/49 Harpers Bazaar

Name-Day Night: 5/49 Right Angle III, 1

The K: ca. early 1945; 2/48 Y & X by Black Sun Press

The Moebius Strip: by 9/46; 3/47 as TO CORRADO CAGLI by Knoedler

Trinacria: 2/46 Harpers Bazaar LXXX as For K

The Green Man: by 9/46; 12/47 Harpers Bazaar LXXXI as In Praise of the Fool

These Days: 1/50 Imagi vol V no 2

The Story of an Olson, and Bad Thing: dated 5-6/6/50; Spring 1951 Origin 1

Adamo Me . . .: early version dated 6/50; Spring 1951 Origin 1

This: ca. 2/51-7/51; Summer 1952 Black Mountain College

Issue, Mood: Summer 1951 Origin 2

Letter for Melville 1951: 17/7/51 Black Mountain College

The Laughing Ones: early version ca. 1950; 1955 FERRINI & OTHERS by Vincent Ferrini

He, who in his abandoned infancy, spoke of Jesus, Caesar, those who beg and Hell: by 30/6/52; Summer 1952 Four Winds 1

The Dry Ode: by 9/2/51; 1951 Golden Goose ser 3, 1

La Preface: by 9/46; 2/48 Y & X by Black Sun Press

The Kingfishers: dated 20/7/49; Summer 1950 Montevallo Review I, 1

ABCs: early 1953 Artisan 2

ABCs (2): 2/53 Origin 8 (IN COLDHELL, IN THICKET)

ABCs (3—for Rimbaud): 2/53 Origin 8

There was a Youth whose Name was Thomas Granger: Spring 1947 Western Review XI, 3

Siena, 1948: Winter 1949 Western Review XIII, 2

Other Than: by 9/2/51; 1951 Golden Goose ser 3, 1

At Yorktown: 2/53 Origin 8

The Praises: by 2/1/50; 12/50 NEW DIRECTIONS XII

La Chute: Summer 1951 Goad I, 1

In Cold Hell, In Thicket: by 9/2/51; 1951 Golden Goose ser 3, 1

Move Over: ca. 1947; 1951 Golden Goose ser 3, 1

A Round & A Canon: by 31/7/51; Fall 1951 Origin 3

The Moon is the Number 18: by 12/1/51; Spring 1951 Origin 1

La Torre: by 26/11/51; 2/53 Origin 8

For Sappho, Back: by 22/6/51; Summer 1951 Montevallo Review I, 2

The Ring of: by 30/6/52, 2/53 Origin 8

An Ode on Nativity: ca. 12/51; Spring 1952 Montevallo Review I, 3

The Leader: by 12/7/52; Nov/Jan 1952/53 Contact 5

To Gerhardt, there among Europe's things . . .: dated 28/6/51; Winter 1951 Origin 4

A Po-sy, a Po-sy: by 12/1/51; Summer 1951 Origin 2

A Discrete Gloss: dated 6/51-1/52; Summer 1952 Origin 6

Concerning Exaggeration, or How, Properly, to Heap Up: by 26/6/51; 2/53 Origin 8

Merce of Egypt: by 4/12/52; 2/53 Origin 8

Knowing All Ways, Including the Transposition of Continents: by 30/6/52; 2/53 Origin 8

The Morning News: by 7/3/50; Summer 1953 Origin 10

I, Mencius, Pupil of the Master . . .: Winter 1954 Black Mountain Review 4

Anecdotes of the Late War: 1955 Black Mountain College

The Death of Europe: by 26/8/54; Summer 1955 Origin 16

Proensa: by 24/9/53; Jan/Apr 1954 Contact 9

The Cause, The Cause: by 3/6/51; Spring 1956 Black Mountain Review 6

Love: by 24/8/54; Autumn 1954 Origin 14

The Motion: by 24/8/54; Autumn 1954 Origin 14

The Pavement: by 24/8/54; Autumn 1954 Origin 14

Asymptotes: Spring 1953 Artisan 2

The Post Virginal: dated 24/5/55; Summer 1962 Measure 3

For a man gone to Stuttgart . . . : Summer 1962 Jargon

Variations done for Gerald Van DeWiele: ca. Spring 1956; Summer 1957 Measure 1

Queen Street Burle-Q: 1/57 Combustion 1

I believe in you . . ..: late 1953 CIV/n 6

The Loves of Anat, 1: 1/57 Combustion 1

Christmas: 1/59 The Nation CLXXXVIII

O'Ryan (1-10): (2) Summer 1955 Black Mountain Review 5; (2, 4, 6, 8, 10) 9/58 White Rabbit Press; (1-10) 9/65 White Rabbit Press

The Lordly and Isolate Satyrs: by 1956; Spring 1958 Evergreen Review I, 4

A Newly Discovered 'Homeric' Hymn: Summer 1956 Origin 19

As the Dead Prey Upon Us: dated 13-16/4/56; Winter 1956-57 Ark II/Moby 1

Moonset, Gloucester, December 1, 1957 . . .: dated 1/12/57; Summer 1959 Partisan Review XXVI

Borne down by the inability to lift . . .: Fall 1961 Outsider I, 1

The Company of Men: dated Christmas 1957; Spring 1959 Evergreen Review II, 8

The Distances: dated 17/10/59; 1960 Yugen 6

(Dencensus spiritus, No. 1): by 9/57; Winter 1958 Measure 2

The year is a great circle . . .: dated 15/1/58; Summer 1962 Measure 3

The Red Fish-of-Bones: 4/62 Poetry C, 1

Of Women: by 1957; Winter 1958 Measure 2

The Americans: by 6/12/61; 1961 Floating Bear 17

turn now & rise: Winter 1965 Niagara Frontier Review 3

Across Space and Time: Winter 1961-62 Set 1

The Allegory of Wealth: 1961 Outburst 1

The Librarian: by 1956; 1/59 Yugen 4

about the dead he sd: 1960 Neon Obit

The Binnacle: ca. Summer 1957; 28/12/61 Albuquerque Review

Place; & Names: dated 5/1/62; 1962 Yugen 8

'West'

      as of Bozeman: 1969 Yugen 6

      Two Poems

            'men are only known in memory . . .': dated 4/63; 1/64 Wild Dog I, 5

            'The Pedens, who re-walked . . .': 1/64 Wild Dog I, 5

      'West' 4 and 5: 5/4/64 Wild Dog 7

      'West' 6: 10/64 Wild Dog II, 10

To Empty the Mind: 1961 Floating Bear 16

Oh! Fa-doo: the enormous success of clerks: ca. 3/64; 7/64 Matter 2

A Note for Anyone Able to: 7/64 Matter 2

pitcher, how: 8/58 Neon/Supplement to Now

Memory, Mind, and Will: dated 4/3/64; 7/64 Matter 2

Buffalo Ode (1-5): (1(4/64 Resuscitator 2; (1-5) 5/65 Rescuscitator 4

you can't use words as ideas: dated 1/10/64; 2/65 Tuftonian Centennial Issue

The Grandfather-Father Poem: dated 1964; 4-5/65 Poetry CVI, 1-2

The Lamp: dated 14/10/64; 10/65 Magazine of Further Studies 2

like a foldout: 4/65 Wild Dog 16

Light is not colour: 7/64 Matter 2

Color is reflective: 1964 Matter 3

color is not the noun: by 1964; 1968 Matter 4

light sits under one's eyes: dated 30/8/68; 4/9/68 Gloucester Daily Times

An Enthusiasm: dated 9/10/65; 16/10/65 Gloucester Daily Times

  A Scream to the Editor: 3/12/65 Gloucester Daily Times

Rocking Meter over Desolation: dated 20/1/68; 26/1/68 Gloucester Daily Times

for my friend: dated 3-4/65; 11/67 Magazine of Further Studies

from the Song of Ullikummi: by Summer 1965; 11/66 City Lights Journal 3

So the Norse: 1966 Before Your Very Eyes

the heart like a clock: dated 21/1/68; 1970 Aries Publications